BRITAIN AND NUCLEAR WEAPONS

By the same author

US INTELLIGENCE AND THE SOVIET STRATEGIC THREAT

EVOLUTION OF NUCLEAR STRATEGY (*forthcoming*)
(Studies in International Security)

BRITAIN AND NUCLEAR WEAPONS

Lawrence Freedman

Published for

THE ROYAL INSTITUTE OF
INTERNATIONAL AFFAIRS

First published 1980 by
THE MACMILLAN PRESS LTD
London and Basingstoke
Companies and representatives
throughout the world

Filmset by Vantage Photosetting Co. Ltd, Southampton and London
Printed in Great Britain by
Billing and Sons Ltd,
Guildford, Worcester and London

British Library Cataloguing in Publication Data

Freedman, Lawrence
   Britain and nuclear weapons
   1. Great Britain – Military policy
   2. Atomic weapons
   I. Title   II. Royal Institute of International Affairs
   355.03'35'41   UA647

   ISBN 0–333–30494–2
   ISBN 0–333–30511–6 (Papermac)

Contents

Acknowledgements   vii

List of Abbreviations   ix

Introduction   xi

1   The Nuclear Bias   1

2   From *Skybolt* to *Polaris*   10

3   The Problem of Strategy   19

4   The Labour Government and Nuclear Weapons
    1964–70   31

5   *Chevaline*   41

6   The Problem of Replacement   52

7   Cruise Missiles *versus* Ballistic Missiles   69

8   Defence Priorities   79

9   Arms Control   86

10 The Strategic Context   101

11 Nuclear Politics in Europe   114

12 Rationales   127

Appendices

1 Submarines   142

2 Characteristics of SLBMs   143

3 Expenditure on Nuclear Weapons (current £m)   144

4 Breakdown of Costs of Nuclear Strategic Forces   145

5 Manpower   146

6 *Polaris* Missile Tests   147

7 Underground Nuclear Tests   148

Notes   149

Index   154

Acknowledgements

It is not possible to thank all those who have helped me with this book, but I would like to express particular gratitude to Charles Douglas-Home, Rear-Admiral Edward Gueritz, Professor Michael Howard, Professor Peter Nailor, Ian Smart and, as ever, my wife for their encouragement and advice.

This book is in part a result of work undertaken for Chatham House's British Foreign Policy Project, which was funded by the Leverhulme Trust.

LAWRENCE FREEDMAN

List of Abbreviations

ABM	Anti-Ballistic Missile
ALCM	Air-Launched Cruise Missile
ANF	Atlantic Nuclear Force
BAOR	British Army of the Rhine
ASW	Anti-Submarine Warfare
CTBT	Comprehensive Test Ban Treaty
GLCM	Ground-Launched Cruise Missile
ICBM	Intercontinental Ballistic Missile
IISS	International Institute for Strategic Studies
IRBM	Intermediate Range Ballistic Missile
MIRV	Multiple Independently-Targetable Re-entry Vehicle
MLF	Multilateral Force
MOD	Ministry of Defence
MRBM	Medium-Range Ballistic Missile
MRV	Multiple Re-entry Vehicle
NATO	North Atlantic Treaty Organisation
NPG	Nuclear Planning Group
NPT	Non-Proliferation Treaty
PTBT	Partial Test Ban Treaty
SALT	Strategic Arms Limitation Talks
SIOP	Single Integrated Operations Plan
SLBM	Submarine-Launched Ballistic Missile
SLCM	Submarine-Launched Cruise Missile
TERCOM	Terrain Contour Matching
TNF	Theatre Nuclear Forces
UN	United Nations

List of Abbreviations

Introduction

I

Plans for a future war assume that, if it should 'go nuclear', Britain could within one day suffer attack from 200 warheads each with an explosive yield equivalent to one million tons of TNT (one megaton). Around the centre of each explosion would be miles of complete devastation, with fire and radiation effects persisting after the blast effects had run their course. Crude calculations can be made of an individual's chances of surviving such an explosion – 20 per cent at a mile from the centre, 40 per cent after three miles and so on, but the margin of error is enormous. The long-term consequences, of lingering radiation or social and economic disruption, are even harder to predict.

The question of whether the Government could do more to improve the survival chances of the population has become a matter of some controversy. After optimism over the potential for Civil Defence in the early 1950s, confidence began to wane in its value until the organisation was virtually disbanded in 1968. What remains is an impressive ability to sound the alarm and monitor the effects of an attack, a capacity to maintain a functioning administrative apparatus, a modicum of law and order in the aftermath and some stockpiles of foodstuffs and other commodities.

The controversy surrounds the question of whether much can be done for the population at large. The official line is that protection should be on a do-it-yourself basis. With some justice it is pointed out that mass evacuations would gain little, because there would be no guaranteed 'safe' place to which to go. People would be encouraged to stay at home and do the best they could in constructing a makeshift shelter in which to stay until the danger

of fallout had passed. However, without a few weeks' warning that
a war could be imminent (recognised as such at the time) there
would not even be enough time to print, let alone distribute, the
necessary manual entitled *Protect and Survive*. The other main
source of instruction would be communications as the crisis
reached its climax from a special wartime broadcasting service.

At Fylingdales in Yorkshire the early warning station will be
first to have notice of an incoming attack. Within $2\frac{1}{2}$ minutes most
of the population should be aware of the 'attack warning red' as
7000 power-operated and 11,000 hand-operated sirens are
sounded along with broadcast messages on television and radio.
Minutes later the first missiles will reach their target and the
people will have to make do as best they can.

II

As little can be done to limit the consequences of nuclear war
should it occur, the policy of Britain since 1945 has been to deter
the employment of nuclear weapons against it by using the threat
of counter-employment. Thus, seven times as much money is
spent each year on preparing to wreak havoc on the Soviet Union
than defending the British population from Soviet nuclear
weapons. To add weight to the threat of retaliation in kind, at
least one submarine carrying 16 *Polaris* missiles is always on
station. Each of the four boats in the *Polaris* flotilla is capable of
inflicting massive destruction on the USSR, with millions of
deaths and injuries. This threat could certainly be augmented
during a crisis lasting a few days, by curtailing the short rest and
maintenance period for a boat at port in between patrols, or by
keeping a boat on station that was due to return to port (extra
supplies are kept on board for such emergencies). Even if there
were only half an hour warning time, this would be long enough
for a submarine stuck at port to prepare its missiles for firing.
However, the theory of strategic deterrence does not permit the
retaliatory force to depend on warning. There must be confidence
that a sufficient part of it will not be caught in a surprise attack,
and will remain able to inflict its terrible retribution.

To reduce the vulnerability to Soviet anti-submarine measures
the *Polaris* boats exploit their mobility moving from the safe, deep
waters around Scotland to the vast expanses of the Atlantic
Ocean. The length of each patrol is irregular, although around

10–12 weeks. Only a few know the route of the patrol. The boat will leave port in such a way as to confuse any waiting Soviet submarines wishing to trail it. At sea everything is done to avoid being noticed: the boat never surfaces and noise is kept down to a minimum; there is a doctor on board capable of performing emergency operations to avoid having to interrupt a patrol for medical reasons; radio silence is maintained so that there can be communications sent to the boat, but it sends no messages in return. The crew are positively vetted when they volunteer for *Polaris* duty. On patrol there has been far less homosexuality, mental illness, drug-taking or tormented consciences than originally expected.

During patrol a constant watch is kept for signs of Soviet submarines. NATO submarines, at least for the moment, are able to detect their Soviet counterparts before they are detected themselves. This allows time for evasive action. In wartime, if evasion was for some reason not possible, the *Polaris* boats could protect themselves against attack using their own torpedoes.

A decision to launch the *Polaris* missiles could only be taken by the Prime Minister. However, Mrs Thatcher could not initiate the launching procedure by herself. This would require the participation of at least one member of the Chiefs of Staff. A civil servant and military officer, with access to the relevant safes and codes, are always on hand. The captain of the submarine would be alerted by headquarters in London; in 15 minutes its missile could be ready for action. On the boat no single individual has all the information relevant to a missile launch, and the critical launch procedures have to be conducted by two senior officers. While the countdown is under way, the captain must keep a key inserted in a box. He can stop the countdown at any stage by removing it. These two officers are capable of launching the missiles of their own volition. The only circumstances in which they are permitted to even consider this are when they have reason to believe that Britain has been devastated by a nuclear attack and no responsible person is in a position to transmit orders to them. They must monitor all possible forms of communication (and there are many) before making any decision. To quote one *Polaris* commander: 'You don't unleash Armageddon on the basis 'of radio silence!'

Each boat carries hundreds of target tapes. The choice between them is made in London, although the captain has his own list in case a missile aborts and another has to be re-targeted to take its place. Once the firing begins there need only be 14 seconds between volleys; even less if the captain is prepared to take some risks with the boat's stability as water rushes in to fill the spaces vacated by the missiles. Once all the missiles are released, the submarine changes mission and prepares to make use of the torpedoes it also carries on board in attacks on the enemy navy. By this time the crew could only assume that little would be left of its own country.

III

It has been a long time since there was a serious debate in Britain on the maintenance of this small national nuclear force. In the late 1950s and early 1960s the issue was at the centre of British politics. The Campaign for Nuclear Disarmament was able to mobilise hundreds of thousands of people in an effort to 'ban the bomb', and managed to put enormous strain on the internal composure of the Labour Party. Perhaps because it was such a divisive issue then, politicians have been wary of raising it since. Until recently there did not seem much need to raise the issue. The nuclear force did not draw attention to itself. No Government came at all close to even seriously thinking about using it, while the cost of its purchase and maintenance represented only a modest portion of the national budget. In the absence of major decisions to be taken on nuclear weapons policy, other issues came to dominate political debate. The nuclear issue was kept hidden, with little official comment on the matter, and secrecy unusually tight even by British standards.

For a number of reasons there has been a recent resurgence in interest in nuclear weapons issues. The advancing years of Britain's *Polaris* fleet has stimulated speculation over the need for, and possible character of, a replacement force. With its allies in the North Atlantic Treaty Organisation (NATO) Britain has shared in the confusion of 1978 over whether to introduce the neutron bomb, and in 1979, the relative decisiveness on the modernisation of the alliance's long-range theatre nuclear forces. In the background there has been a deep, and increasingly bitter, argument over whether or not the strategic balance is tilting in favour of the Soviet Union, away from the United States; an argument reflected in the glacial progress of the Strategic Arms Limitation Talks (SALT).

This book is mainly concerned with Britain's own strategic nuclear force – its past development and the issues surrounding its replacement. It begins with a history of the force, concentrating on the past two decades. In discussing decision-making on the nuclear force, the book will describe the strategic, technological, political and economic factors that have shaped the development of the force. For the more recent period the scope of the analysis is widened. A full nuclear weapons policy includes a range of issues. In addition to its own nuclear force, Britain hosts many American aircraft and nuclear submarines, and will soon accommodate some 160 ground-launched cruise missiles. It participates in a number of arms-control efforts devoted to the key NATO meetings where policy for the alliance as a whole is determined. Thus one objective of this book is to put the current replacement issue in the context of the other nuclear debates that have preoccupied NATO in recent years, and the overall state of the East–West military balance.

The replacement question itself can be divided into two: whether it is worth Britain having a nuclear force at all; and the most appropriate force, if the answer to the first part of the question is positive. As will be seen, I am more confident in my views on the second of these matters than on the first. I have attempted to provide a reasonable if critical account of the arguments employed in the debate. It may be that the method I have used is not wholly fair to the more radical opponents of the nuclear force because their case has rarely penetrated the rather exclusive circle of decision-makers whose deliberations provide the central focus of this study.

The agnosticism of this study is partly a reflection of a determination to provide a book of description and analysis rather than advocacy. In the past, with a few notable exceptions, neither the process nor the substance of British defence policy has been discussed in the sort of detail that is so common in the United States. I hope this book will demonstrate that neither the sensitivity of the issues nor the Official Secrets Act need prevent a serious and informed public debate on the crucial questions of national security.

1   The Nuclear Bias

A strategic nuclear weapons programme decided upon in 1980 will not be ready until the 1990s, and could be playing a role in Britain's defence until well into the next century. While we may think responsible policy on the nuclear programme requires some attempt to anticipate the strategic environment of the twenty-first century, it is more likely that, as in the past, the relevant decisions will reflect current pressures and interests rather than speculation over the future.

The first moves, early in the last war, to press ahead with the investigation of the military potential of recent discoveries in atomic fission were taken because of a fear that the Germans were probably engaged in similar investigations. When it was agreed in 1942 to subsume the British effort in the much larger American 'Manhattan project', it was because the need to construct atom bombs, before Germany did so, overrode concerns over national sovereignty. The post-war British programme was determined by the assumption that a major power had little choice but to develop the most modern weapons available, and by the irritating fact that the Americans ended the post-war partnership in atomic research somewhat abruptly. Aggrieved that the United States was not willing to reward Britain's wartime selflessness in assisting the American programme, it was felt that the only option was to go it alone and become a self-sufficient nuclear power.[1]

This decision was taken at a time of great uncertainty over the shape of world politics. By the time of the test of Britain's first atomic device at Monte Bello, Australia, on 3 October 1952, the international scene was much clearer. The United States and Britain were now allies again, joined with other major Western nations in the North Atlantic Treaty Organisation (NATO). The potential enemy was the Soviet Union, controlling Eastern

1

Europe and itself a nuclear power. Britain's capacity to continue
to play a major world role was coming to be doubted. The
assumption of the mid-1940s, that the construction of large,
reliable and impressive stockpiles of nuclear weapons would be a
slow and tortuous development had been proved false. By 1952,
the United States was accumulating an imposing arsenal and was
rapidly developing the relevant technology in all directions. By
the mid-1950s their bomb-makers had progressed from atomic
fission to thermonuclear fusion and were able to manufacture
explosions ranging from the equivalent of a few thousand tons to
millions of tons of TNT. New vehicles, aircraft and missiles, were
being designed to extend the ease, speed and range of delivery.
The appearance of the Soviet Union as the second nuclear power
in 1949 suggested that only countries able to devote the necessary
industrial resources and scientific ingenuity to bomb development could continue to keep to the front of this particular race.

The British Government did not want to drop out of the race
but increasingly was forced to recognise that it could not carry on
unaided. During the decade Britain was successful in achieving
American help to sustain its nuclear effort. One important con-
tributory factor to this success was an explicit nuclear bias in
NATO's strategy, that had come about partly at Britain's
prompting and which encouraged a policy of interdependence for
the alliance's two nuclear powers.

NATO STRATEGY

At the start of the 1950s British defence policy reflected a marked
aversion to nuclear weapons. When, early in the Korean War,
President Truman hinted that the United States was contemplating the use of atomic bombs, the British Prime Minister Clement
Attlee hurried over the Atlantic to warn him that these weapons
were seen in Britain very much as instruments of last resort. The
Labour Government was prepared, at some sacrifice to its domestic economic and social policies, to engage in a major rearmament
programme as a response to the general Soviet offensive that, it
was believed, lay behind the invasion of South Korea. But it was
conventional forces that were stressed in this programme: only

slight stimulus was given to the development of Britain's nuclear capability. The concentration on the weapons of the last World War, rather than those of the new atomic age, was based on the realistic assumption that any special strategic advantages that might have accrued from the West's atomic bombs were gradually being diminished as the Soviet Union built up its own arsenal. The importance of a British bomb would be its capacity to deter, through threat of retaliation, any use of Soviet bombs against the British Isles.

With a change to a Conservative Government in 1951 the nuclear aversion in British defence policy became transformed into a nuclear bias. This bias was very much favoured by the Prime Minister Winston Churchill. He had encouraged the development of the atomic bomb during the war and, while in opposition, had identified the American atomic monopoly as the major reason why the Soviet Union had not taken over the whole of Western Europe during the unsettled period of the late 1940s. Returning to office in 1951 he was impressed by the strides that had been taken in the development and production of nuclear weapons in the United States since 1945, while alarmed that Britain was still incurring a heavy financial burden in building up its conventional forces.

In 1952 the Chiefs of Staff produced a Global Strategy Paper which argued that much more reliance should be placed on nuclear threats in containing the expansion of Soviet power. The policy reflected a set of widely held assumptions. The destructive power of nuclear weapons was considered so great that no nation would dare to provoke a war in which there was the slightest risk of it becoming the victim of an attack using them. There was no plausible defence against these weapons. It would require a major effort and expense to develop sufficient nuclear capability to destroy the Soviet Union as a viable society, but far less than an attempt to match the vast conventional forces at the disposal of the Kremlin. If it was made clear that nuclear weapons would be used in NATO's defence then it was felt that the Soviet Union would be inhibited from launching an attack, particularly while the West still enjoyed a significant relative, if no longer absolute, superiority over the East in the quantity and quality of its nuclear stockpile.

In 1952 this was a policy that only the United States could

implement, for Britain was only just preparing to test its first atom bomb. It was not until 1953, with a new Republican Administration equally anxious over the economic strains caused by a large defence budget, that the United States began to move in the direction desired by Britain. In 1953 the nuclear bias was formally introduced into NATO strategy. This 'New Look', as it was described, was publicised in a famous speech of January 1954 by Secretary of State John Foster Dulles. He stressed the importance of a 'great capacity to retaliate, instantly, by means and at places of our own choosing'. In the future, rather than fight communist aggression on its own terms with strong local conventional forces, the response would take the form of a punishing attack, of a magnitude, and at targets, appropriate to the crime.

The British applauded this approach, and put extra effort into their own nuclear programme so as to support this Western strategy. In 1955, before the RAF was ready to deploy its first atom bombs, a decision to develop hydrogen (thermonuclear) bombs was announced. In late 1956 there was the start of an operational nuclear capability. The next year, the trend in British, and NATO, strategy was confirmed in an uncompromising manner in the Defence White Paper, presented by Duncan Sandys, the Minister of Defence.[2] It emphasised the commitment to nuclear weapons as the most effective deterrent to war and means of waging it, should it occur. On this basis, large conventional forces were no longer required. A reduction of these forces allowed for the termination of national service and a cut in the defence budget.

In 1958, Sandys made it clear that the West now had little choice but to rely on nuclear deterrence:

> . . . it must be well understood that if Russia were to launch a major attack on [the Western powers] even with conventional forces only, they would have to hit back with strategic nuclear weapons. In fact, the strategy of NATO is based on the frank recognition that a full-scale Soviet attack could not be repelled without resort to a massive nuclear bombardment of the sources of power in Russia.

Soon, the report noted, while not comparing in total size to the US force, 'when fully equipped with megaton weapons, the British bomber force will in itself constitute a formidable deterrent'.[3]

As Britain had, at one point early in the war, been ahead of the United States in atom bomb research it never seriously occurred to the responsible British politicians and officials that any special rationale was needed to justify staying in the business. It had been assumed, in the immediate post-war period, that without a British contribution the Americans would not have enough bombs to cover all Soviet targets. By the 1950s, after a faster-than-expected growth in the American arsenal, the British argument shifted to the need to attack targets of low priority to the United States, for example the bases of Soviet medium-range aircraft, missiles and submarines. In addition, if the West was to rely on the deterrent effect of nuclear power, then it seemed only proper that a country of Britain's status should participate fully in the construction and implementation of this strategy. In 1955, Harold Macmillan, then Minister of Defence, argued against the 'dangerous doctrine' of relying solely on the US nuclear deterrent to the exclusion of the British contribution:

> Politically it surrenders our power to influence American policy and then, strategically and tactically it equally deprives us of any influence over the selection of targets and the use of our vital striking forces. The one, therefore weakens our prestige and our influence in the world, and the other might imperil our safety.[4]

Less explicit, but always present, was the fear of excessive dependence on the United States. Britain could be left dangerously exposed should there be some dramatic change in America's attitude towards a modern version of isolationism.

The Suez debacle of 1956 might have been expected to encourage the case for more effective conventional forces, and a more honest assessment of Britain's international position. However, hurt pride, a bit of nuclear sabre-rattling by the Soviet Union towards the end of the crisis and the opposition of the United States, reinforced the enthusiasm for a nuclear force that, it was believed, would increase Britain's freedom of manoeuvre. In addition to the established sense of responsibility of a major power in contributing to Western defence, a new theme – that of nuclear weapons raising Britain's declining international status – came to be stressed. The assertion of 'independence' became something of a preoccupation. This was unfortunate because the idea that nuclear weapons were to be a determining factor in the international hierarchy was an illusion (and one that it was best not to encourage), and also because Britain was entering a period in which full nuclear independence, in the sense of complete self-sufficiency if not control, was becoming beyond its means. This sort of rhetoric also contradicted the actual thrust of British policy. This had been to actively seek a large measure of interdependence with the United States, not to produce a nuclear capability in order to 'stand alone' but to contribute to the particular NATO strategy it had promoted, the development of which it wished to continue to influence.

ANGLO-AMERICAN COLLABORATION

While Britain considered a capacity to actually engage in independent nuclear operation essential, the real value of its forces was seen in the context of its preferred NATO doctrine, enhancing its position within the alliance, and strengthening its hand in the unusually close bilateral relationship it enjoyed with the United States. Indeed, much diplomatic effort during the 1950s went into encouraging forms of interdependence with the United States. The assumption was that the development and production of nuclear weapons remained a difficult and expensive business, so that the two main Western powers concerned would be wise to pool resources. At least in some of its aspects the provision of NATO's nuclear deterrent would be a collaborative exercise. There would be a genuine exchange of information and materials, not simply a one-way transfer from the United States to Britain.

Cooperation of this sort had been a feature of the war-time atom bomb project, although Britain was very much the junior partner. The passage of the Atomic Energy Act by the US Congress in 1946, one of the aims of which was to prevent the dissemination of nuclear secrets to other nations, impeded the continuation of nuclear collaboration.

In a series of frustrating negotiations in the 1940s, remarkable mainly for how little they disrupted overall Anglo-American relations, the United States gave little away, pointing to Britain's strategic vulnerability and lax security to justify the minimum of transfer of the fruits of its research and experience. The British bargaining chips, which included a notional right to veto any use of the bomb (left over from a war-time agreement between Churchill and Roosevelt) and a number of areas of high research competence, were conceded in a futile attempt to get the Americans to honour past obligations. The result was a bomb more 'independent' than originally anticipated, an achievement which strengthened Britain's hand when negotiations resumed on co-operation in the mid-1950s.

A more permissive US Atomic Energy Act in 1954 made possible limited exchanges, but it was not until the act was further amended in 1958 that extensive arrangements for collaboration became possible. With the explosion of its first thermonuclear (hydrogen) bomb in May 1957 Britain had demonstrated that it was becoming a mature nuclear power. President Eisenhower therefore felt able to propose amendment to the 1954 Act so as to permit a greater exchange with countries which had 'made substantial progress in the development of atomic weapons'. By July 1958 Congress has passed the necessary legislation and the next month an Anglo-American agreement 'for Cooperation on the Uses of Atomic Energy for Mutual Defence Purposes' came into effect. In 1959 this agreement was amended, taking it beyond similar arrangements with other allies, to put Britain in a special and elevated position with regard to cooperation. The understanding was quite general and permissive rather than specific and mandatory. The details were filled in as time went on.

The United States accepted this because of the virtues of a division of labour in an area where talents and resources remained scarce. Information on British techniques would provide a useful check on the adequacy of its own, and on occasion might allow for important innovations. British nuclear materials might also be used to make up for shortfalls in American supplies. In return Britain would receive details on all components of a military nuclear capability, including delivery vehicles, as well as nuclear submarine fuels.[5]

The British, therefore, in the 1950s were aiming for an 'independent' nuclear deterrent only in the sense of national control over its use. There was no pretence that there was to be complete self-sufficiency in its development. However, in accepting American assistance, there was a belief that this was provided in the context of a mutual interdependence, in which Britain was offering something in return.

SKYBOLT

It was in the area of delivery systems that the most visible, and politically controversial, dependence developed on US technology. The first purpose-built delivery systems, the V-bombers, were of British design and manufacture, but by the time they were coming into service in 1958 it had become apparent that to continue developing systems both technically advanced and all-British would be an immense strain. In particular, it would be very difficult to follow the movement from bombers to missiles, already evident in both the super-powers. The *Blue Steel* stand-off missile, designed to ease the V-bombers' enormous problems in penetrating Soviet air defences, was of British design. However, when in 1957 it was decided to develop an intermediate-range ballistic missile, *Blue Streak*, for the next generation of delivery vehicles rather than a new supersonic bomber, an injection of American technology was required. Although not publicly disclosed at the time, *Blue Streak*'s motor and internal guidance system were derived from American blueprints for an early design, later overtaken, for America's *Atlas* missile.

Yet even with this help there were signs that technology was moving too fast for Britain to keep abreast of the capabilities of the super-powers. It became clear that *Blue Streak* was going to be obsolete even before it was operational. The growth in Soviet offensive capabilities would make the new weapon, placed in fixed launch sites, vulnerable to a surprise attack, despite being placed in underground, hardened shelters. Liquid-fuelled, it was slow and awkward in preparation for launch.

In 1960, having spent £65 million on the project, and aware of a probably eventual bill of £600 million for an inadequate system, the Government cancelled *Blue Streak*. If Britain was to have any sort of credible nuclear capability it was necessary to accept even greater dependence on the United States. It was announced in April 1960 that it would purchase the American *Skybolt* air-launched ballistic missile. With a British warhead, *Skybolt* would be fitted to the V-bombers to extend their useful life until the 1970s.

Britain had little equivalent to offer the Americans in return for this generosity. There was one major bargaining card: its geographic position within easy range of the Soviet Union. Before the

United States had a large and secure intercontinental bomber and missile force, it required European bases in order to threaten its 'potential enemy'. Britain had been a willing host to American strategic bombers since the Berlin crisis of 1948. In 1958 it was agreed that American *Thor* intermediate range missiles were to be placed in Britain, though the British were to be allowed a say in any decision to use them and they were seen, partly, as a stop-gap until the British *Blue Streak* was ready. In November 1960, it was announced that the United States was to use Holy Loch in Scotland as a base for its *Polaris* nuclear submarines. The provision of this facility was seen as an exchange for access to *Skybolt*. No major new conditions were to be attached to the use either of America's new base or Britain's new missile.

Britain had at last managed to secure close ties with the United States in nuclear affairs. They were sharing technology, materials, information and systems. There was close cooperation in the technical assessment of the Soviet nuclear and missile-testing programme. Both used the British Isles as a base. Both shared the same basic approach to the role of nuclear weapons in NATO strategy. Both were negotiating with the Soviet Union on the question of a ban on nuclear testing. Nevertheless, within a year of the agreement on *Skybolt*, strains were beginning to show as a result of the underlying lack of symmetry in the Anglo-American relationship and a new divergence over strategic doctrine.

2 From *Skybolt* to *Polaris*

The period of the late 1950s and early 1960s was one of great turmoil in weapons technology and strategic thinking. Increasingly the wisdom of the nuclear bias of NATO's strategy was questioned as the Soviet Union made impressive strides in the development of its own nuclear capability. Serious doubts were raised as to whether it was realistic to expect an American President to initiate a nuclear war, with the probable consequence of the devastation of his own country, in the event of conventional attack by the Soviet Union on Western Europe.

The initial response to this problem by NATO governments was to accentuate the alliance's nuclear bias by developing small, 'tactical', nuclear weapons for battlefield use, to be employed almost as if they were conventional weapons. It soon became evident that, whatever their value, they offered no panacea to the basic problem. Exercises in the mid-1950s demonstrated that their use on any scale, even if only by NATO, would have appalling effects on any civilians close to the fighting (likely to be most of the German population). Once the Warsaw Pact obtained its own tactical nuclear weapons, the stalemate was merely established at a lower level. There was no obvious way for NATO to use nuclear weapons to gain a decisive strategic advantage. In that case any threat of nuclear use to deter Soviet aggression seemed quite empty. A credibility gap emerged at the heart of NATO strategy.

The extent of the Soviet challenge was not fully appreciated until October 1957, when the Soviet Union, after beating the United States to the first test of an intercontinental ballistic missile (ICBM), achieved the first launch of an artificial satellite *Sputnik I*. The American mood changed from complacency to panic, encouraged by the Russian leader Nikita Khruschev with a series of mischievous (and unwarranted) boasts about the extent of his country's lead in the development and production of long-range rockets. The response of the Eisenhower Administration was diplomatically sound, if lacking in rigorous strategic logic. It was unwilling to unravel the past decade's work in forging a coherent Atlantic Alliance around a common strategy, even if it did rely unduly on nuclear weapons. The threat might be less convincing than before, but some risk of a nuclear riposte to any aggression remained, and that was probably sufficient to deter any Soviet adventures.

THE NEW STRATEGY

By way of contrast, the response of the Kennedy Administration, which came to power in January 1961, was strong on strategic logic but lacking in diplomatic tact. There were four key elements to this response. The first priority was to ensure that the Soviet Union could not disarm the United States in a surprise attack. That meant that weapons had to be either mobile or protected.

A second and related requirement was the need to ensure that any nuclear use was a deliberate decision and not forced on a US President by the exigencies of a military crisis. It would not do for the super-powers to feel obliged to respond, without hesitation, to the first warning of an enemy nuclear attack, or even enemy preparations for a nuclear attack. If both super-powers entered a crisis with fingers close to the trigger, for fear of the disastrous consequences of being beaten to the draw, it would be difficult to keep calm and keep the situation under control. This led to the requirement of retaliatory forces that would not have to be launched on warning, but could 'ride out' an attack. It also became advisable not to make the other side too jumpy by mounting a convincing threat to his means of retaliation.

Third, more thought had to go into methods of using nuclear weapons when and if this became necessary. Simply punishing aggression made little sense when the aggressor could return the punishment. It was more advisable to consider forms of employment that would bring some military benefits or else serve as a form of bargaining, attempting by limited strikes to underline the

dangers of what might follow if diplomatic means were not found
to stop the fighting. To engage in such a subtle nuclear strategy,
firm control would be needed.

Finally, the nuclear bias in NATO strategy should be reversed.
The Soviet success in neutralising the nuclear deterrent should be
acknowledged. Henceforth, the most efficient use of resources
would be in building up conventional forces to match those of the
Warsaw Pact. The United States put a lot of effort into demonstrating to its allies that it had exaggerated Warsaw Pact strength
and that a convincing conventional option was well within reach.

THE EUROPEAN REACTION

The Europeans were unconvinced by these arguments and unim-
pressed by the panoply of new concepts and sophisticated analyti-
cal techniques Robert McNamara, President Kennedy's Secretary of Defense, deployed in their presentation. The allies' ire was
mainly directed at the attempt to reverse the nuclear bias. In part
this was due to the fact that a nuclear strategy is much less
expensive than a conventional strategy (especially when largely
subsidised by the United States). The main concern was over the
trend in American thinking towards treating conventional war in
Europe as tolerable, in a way that nuclear war could not be, taking
it for granted that a Soviet invasion using conventional forces only
carried slight danger of nuclear retaliation. Yet with recent
experience of a conventional war being waged in the centre of
Europe, America's allies considered this only barely less attractive than nuclear war and something that had to be deterred.
Their suspicion was that the desire to improve conventional forces
was more to spare America undue sacrifice than to bolster the
deterrent. They feared that in its efforts to reduce the nuclear risks
to itself, the United States was increasing the conventional (and
'tactical' nuclear) risks to Western Europe.

This suspicion was sharpened by the emphasis the Americans
were placing on keeping firm control over NATO's nuclear
deterrent, even in its reduced role. The desire to have only one
centre of nuclear decision-making – in Washington – meant that
the relevant decisions would reflect American rather than European interests.

THE BRITISH POSITION

All this put Britain in an exceptionally awkward position. Since the start of the cold war British Governments had worked hard to tie the United States as closely as possible to the defence of Europe. It had stressed the coincidence of interests among the Atlantic powers, demonstrating this through its own special relationship with the United States. Its nuclear strategy was largely based on this belief in interdependence. The bickering within the alliance on nuclear strategy therefore left Britain embarrassingly exposed: it needed US help to stay in the nuclear business yet the most convincing rationale for a British nuclear force went against current American doctrine.

The British Government had come to present the nuclear force as a European contribution, which the Americans would appreciate, to the burden of providing the West's nuclear deterrent. Now the American Government was emphasising the need to build up the alliance's conventional forces, Here it expected a major European effort while it took care of nuclear forces. Moreover, a reading of British statements on the role of its nuclear force could lead to the conclusion that part of its value might be in forcing the American hand in a crisis, which is exactly what the new Administration believed would be inimical to efficient crisis management. Any British plea for an independent capacity to initiate nuclear hostilities implied a lack of trust of American motives somewhat discourteous when depending on American hardware to create this 'independent' capacity. Even if the United States could be persuaded to allow Britain special privileges in this area, the worth of the exercise was diminished to the British public by such withering comments as those of Robert McNamara in July 1962 when he described 'limited nuclear capabilities, operating independently' as 'dangerous, expensive, prone to obsolescence and lacking in credibility as a deterrent'.

The American insistence on the desirability of a nuclear monopoly for itself, had obvious and worrisome implications for future Anglo-American nuclear cooperation. In practice the American strictures on this matter were mainly directed at France, which was just beginning to develop its own nuclear capability. This clash between France and the United States was potentially disruptive, as events were to prove. A French Government that was being picked upon for its nuclear pretensions would not look kindly on visible favouritism by the United States towards Britain. Stressing its links with the United States, while others in Europe were loosening theirs, did not provide a good background to Britain's application for membership of the European Economic Community.

There were elements in the British Government sympathetic to the idea of an *entente nucléaire* with France, the most realistic proposal in the early 1960s for a European deterrent. Indeed it was widely assumed that the European Community, once Britain entered, would begin to develop a military identity. Furthermore, the effort to develop a 'force de frappe' was straining France's economy and scientific resources. It might have welcomed British assistance in the provision of technology and nuclear materials, or the collaborative production of modern delivery vehicles to replace the French *Mirage-IV* bombers along with the British V-bombers. France, on the other hand, did not at the time have much to offer Britain.

Moves in this direction, by going against America's policy of restricting the flow of nuclear information to France, would in some areas have contravened the Anglo-American agreements on nuclear cooperation. In addition, the pride of both France and Britain in their nuclear independence made it difficult to raise the issue. However, the main difficulty was that the hints dropped by the British Government as to its interests in collaboration with France were largely used to create a 'France card' for the purposes of bargaining with the United States, rather than to offer an incentive to a leading and wary member of the European Community to ease the way for Britain's membership.

In the event, Britain was unable to use this 'France card' to prevent serious disruption in its nuclear cooperation with the United States. Furthermore, it only proved possible to repair the damage and stay in the nuclear business by demanding special treatment from the Americans. Its success with these demands emphasised Britain's preference for close relations across the Atlantic Ocean to those across the Channel, especially when the Americans had so much more to offer, by way of readily available, advanced technology, than the French.

NASSAU

The crisis with the United States grew out of an element in its new strategy that, superficially at least, was not controversial in NATO. The main property that Robert McNamara looked for in a nuclear delivery vehicle was an ability to survive an enemy surprise attack. On this criterion missiles scored well against bombers because they offered small targets to surprise attack and could either be placed in protected underground shelters or moved around deep under the sea in submarines. Bombers, on the other hand, were vulnerable to attack while on the ground. Survival could only be assured if they were kept on a state of continued airborne alert, which was extremely expensive. Against this the bomber enthusiasts argued that they could carry a larger payload and deliver it with greater accuracy than could missiles.

Whatever the respective merits of bombers and missiles it became apparent that *Skybolt*, the missile upon which the future of the British nuclear deterrent depended, managed to combine the disadvantages of both. It required a vulnerable aircraft for a launch platform, yet had all the limitations of a missile when it reached its target. This, plus a series of technical problems, made this missile uniquely unattractive and a candidate for scrapping, especially when the ground- and sea-launched missile programmes (*Minuteman* and *Polaris*) were going so well.

On 7 November 1962 the Kennedy Administration decided to scrap *Skybolt*. The next day McNamara informed the British of his decision. The failure of the British to anticipate this decision, or of the Americans to anticipate the horrified reaction of the British when it was announced, remains a remarkable example of miscommunication between close allies.[1]

The Americans believed that they had given their allies ample warning that *Skybolt* was in trouble, even during the Eisenhower Administration. The British had not noticed the signals: their refusal to take account of the possibility of cancellation in their plans can only be explained by confidence in the capacity of the American military–industrial complex to push through a favoured weapons programme against the doubts of responsible officials and in Washington's sensitivity to British interests. The consequences of cancellation seemed so damaging that the Government managed to convince itself that it would not happen.

For its part the American Government did not yet fully appreciate the suspicions surrounding its intentions in Europe. British sensibilities had already been bruised by disparaging remarks from Dean Acheson as to Britain's role in the world and the lack of full consultation during the recent Cuban missile crisis. Now the Administration was seen to be using Britain's dependence on the United States for a delivery system as a crude means of forcing it out of a nuclear capability. Even if that was not its intention, the abrupt manner of cancellation had illuminated the extent of dependence at a time when public rhetoric in Britain was extolling the virtues of independence.

On 18 December 1962, a week after the public announcement of *Skybolt*'s cancellation, President Kennedy and Prime Minister Macmillan met in Nassau. As the United States wished only to terminate *Skybolt*, and not its close links with Britain, it proved possible to organise a compromise which, however, damaged Britain's chances of joining the European Community, though to what extent remains unclear. Despite the fact that De Gaulle had already made clear his scepticism as to British credentials for membership of the EEC, Macmillan did hope that a nuclear deal would not unduly aggravate the situation. After Nassau, the Americans offered France a similar deal to that achieved by Britain. De Gaulle, however, was not to be mollified by what appeared to him as a patronising gesture. American help would have certainly been of enormous practical benefit, but to jump at it would have damaged the dignity of France (and incidentally revealed the poor state of its own nuclear programme). What is clear is that the agreement reached at Nassau put Britain's nuclear force on a far more sound basis than it would have been had the *Skybolt* programme continued.

There was some discussion of a formula to keep *Skybolt* alive, but the missile was now discredited and to continue with it would have undermined the credibility of the British force. Alternative air-launched missiles, such as the *Hound Dog*, could not perform a strategic role. There was only one serious alternative and that was the *Polaris* submarine-launched ballistic missile (SLBM).

Britain could have opted for *Polaris* instead of *Skybolt* in 1960. As a virtually invulnerable system it was recognised at the time as being a better long-term prospect than an air-launched force. One reason why it had not been chosen in 1960 was that the time required to build a submarine fleet to carry it would mean reliance on the V-bombers during a period when they would face increasing difficulty in penetrating Soviet air defences. *Polaris* was not ruled out for the 1970s, but an interim solution was required.

A more important reason was that purchase of *Polaris* would have confused the delicate balance of service responsibilities in Britain. Up to this point the Royal Air Force had been responsible for the British nuclear force. Nuclear deterrence came naturally to Bomber Command, the traditions of which were bound up with the strategic applications of air power. The Royal Navy, on the other hand, while it was well informed on *Polaris*, had no tradition of this sort of operation and the First Sea Lord (Lord Louis Mountbatten) was unconvinced of the need for a national deterrent. A new generation of aircraft carriers was of much greater interest, continuing its established task patrolling vital sea routes. An underwater nuclear deterrent would be an expensive distraction. *Skybolt* pleased both services, and so made up in bureaucratic convenience what it lacked in strategic quality.

In December 1962 it had to be *Polaris*. The Prime Minister made it clear that he wanted it on the same terms as *Skybolt*: Britain would purchase the missiles but manufacture the warheads and the launch platform, though help would be appreciated in their design. The difficulty came in reconciling the preferential treatment accorded Britain at a time when a dominant theme in American strategic doctrine was to deny its allies any capacity for independent nuclear decision.

The 'independence' of the deterrent had become something of a British fixation, so there was little positive response to American suggestions that the provision of *Polaris* should only be in the context of a multilateral fleet, also involving France and Germany. At the time, ideas were being developed in the US State Department for such a multilateral force as a means of satisfying European demands for a say in nuclear decision-making. These plans were only half-formed in December 1962 and the British did not believe that the Americans took them really seriously. Nevertheless, references to making these forces 'available for inclusion in a NATO multilateral nuclear force' did appear in the final communiqué, as did a firmer and more immediate commitment to assign the British forces to NATO and target them in accordance with NATO plans. It was stated that 'these British forces will be used for the purposes of international defence of the Western Alliance in all circumstances'. However Macmillan ensured the insertion of a crucial qualifier: 'except where Her Majesty's Government may decide that supreme national interests are at stake'.

After Nassau, the future of the British strategic nuclear force was more secure than ever before, employing the most advanced American technology, yet firmly under national control. The general argument with the Americans over strategy, and the publicity given to Britain's dependence on American missiles with the *Skybolt* affair, exposed the underlying weakness of the rationale that had been developed during the 1950s to support the nuclear force.

3 The Problem of Strategy

A force of submarine-launched missiles was ideal for a small nuclear power. Against McNamara's list of disadvantages of limited nuclear capabilities, Britain's *Polaris* missiles came out remarkably well. They were neither particularly expensive nor 'prone to obsolescence'. McNamara's strictures concerning the danger and lack of credibility of independent nuclear forces assumed vulnerability to surprise attack. This could encourage crisis instability, in which both sides would have an incentive to launch a pre-emptive attack, lest its retaliatory forces get caught on the ground in a disarming strike. The *Polaris* force met this objection. It could not be easily destroyed in a surprise attack and nor was there an incentive for the enemy to attempt to do so, as *Polaris* was only good for crude retaliation, lacking the accuracy for strikes against the enemy's own strategic forces. In the new jargon of strategic studies, *Polaris* was an exemplary 'second-strike' weapon.

These virtues also limited the role the force could play in any hostilities. It was very much a 'last resort' weapon, to be held in reserve until all other options, military and diplomatic, had been exhausted. There would be no pressure to employ the forces early, because they could remain safe underwater. They lacked the accuracy to attack high-value military targets, and were most suitable for the destruction of cities, an event that would probably involve everyone in a general cataclysm. These were forces best held in reserve.

There is much to the argument that any use of nuclear weapons, even if ostensibly precise and discriminating, cannot avoid the risk of suicidal consequences and is therefore a matter of last resort. However, during the 1950s NATO strategy had come to depend on convincing the Soviet Union that any serious breach of the European peace was quite likely to result in a nuclear war. Part of this strategy had been to leave the alliance with precious few alternative options other than nuclear strikes to meet any large-scale aggression should it occur, which is why the opponents of this strategy found it so alarming. In its new approach, the Kennedy Administration argued for a set of serious options below the nuclear threshold. The final clause of the Nassau Agreement notes agreement concerning the importance of a 'non-nuclear sword' as well as a 'nuclear shield', and therefore both sides 'increasing the effectiveness of their conventional forces on a world-wide basis'..

Not a lot was done by Britain in fulfilment of the pledge. In 1961, during the Berlin crisis of that year, there had been a reversal of the radical cut-backs in conventional forces initiated by Duncan Sandys in 1957. Britain's military manpower was stretched by the need to fulfil a variety of colonial and post-colonial commitments outside of Europe. Even when a Labour Government more sympathetic to the American arguments took over in 1964, economic conditions did not permit any serious expansion of conventional capabilities. Nevertheless, NATO did eventually adopt a new doctrine, known as 'flexible response', in 1967 which accepted that nuclear weapons would only be introduced in the event of an attack after conventional means had failed, and strategic weapons only after the 'theatre' nuclear weapons, based on the continent, had been brought into play. While the move to this doctrine made only a slight impression on NATO's force structure it had the result of confirming nuclear weapons as something to be employed only in the most extreme circumstances.

The American suspicion of nuclear weapons embraced the 'theatre' or 'tactical' as well as the 'strategic' variety. Thousands of short-range 'tactical' nuclear weapons, conceived of as providing a massive supplement to conventional firepower, had arrived in Europe. One feature of the 1957 policy had been to encourage the British Army of the Rhine (BAOR) to take this route. In 1960 BAOR received American *Honest John* and *Corporal* short-range missiles, the warheads of which were under American custody, only to be used with American permission. Britain did, in addition, possess an independent capability at this level with a number of strike aircraft, such as the *Canberra* and *Buccaneer* bombers.

The British, American and other NATO forces found tactical planning with these weapons to be extremely difficult, because of uncertainties over whether they would be allowed to use them; over the general difficulties of command and control in the field; and over the strain on soldiers fighting in nuclear conditions of high confusion and great attrition. There was no self-evident way to use them to effect without causing or provoking major damage to one's own side. Most Europeans doubted whether a 'limited' nuclear war was feasible, and were not sure whether they wished to encourage the idea that it was, as any sense of the inevitability of escalation to all-out nuclear war might help to restrain the Soviet Union from experimenting with limited strikes of its own. In addition, they disliked the idea that Europe could become a nuclear battlefield while the super-powers escaped virtually un-scathed and resented that this might be considered merely a 'tactical' matter in the United States. Nevertheless, they favoured the presence of these weapons in Europe as involving a clear commitment of American nuclear weapons to the defence of Europe. It was the link with the 'strategic' forces that was the positive feature, not the illusory similarity with conventional forces.

It was out of recognition of the political role of tactical nuclear weapons, as symbols of the American guarantee, that the Kennedy Administration made no attempt to remove them. However, instinctively they distrusted these weapons, anxious lest early use, prompted by the exigencies of a particularly dangerous situation during a battle, might trigger a general nuclear war prematurely. If not quite weapons of last resort they were of penultimate resort, and the reduced attention they received during the 1960s was yet another indication of the growing nuclear aversion in NATO strategy after the years of nuclear bias.

THE MULTILATERAL FORCE

At Nassau the Americans had contemplated one particular role for the British force: to form a key component of a multilateral force (MLF), designed more to cope with political problems within the alliance than threats from the Soviet Union. This idea had been around in a variety of guises since the Eisenhower Administration, and was kept alive by enthusiasts in the US State

Department. The original stimulus had been the hundreds of medium-range Soviet missiles and aircraft facing Western Europe. It was felt that the Europeans would want to ensure that these forces were being targeted and that this could be done with a European-based force in which all the allies could participate. As the idea developed it came to focus on the danger that if the non-nuclear allies felt left out of this key area of NATO activities, they (particularly West Germany) might seek to obtain a nuclear capability of their own. A proposal eventually emerged for a fleet of 25 surface vessels, each carrying eight *Polaris* missiles and with a crew taken from at least three of the participating nations, all of which would finance the project.

Apart from West Germany, few in Europe were anything other than sceptical because of the cumbersome nature of the proposed force and because it would not solve the basic problem of control over nuclear weapons. Multiple crews and multiple vetoes would lead more to paralysis than decisive action in a crisis. In Britain the whole scheme was generally considered nonsense. Surface ships would be vulnerable to conventional attack and liable to get involved in awkward incidents at sea. The Royal Navy was aghast at the thought of mixed-nationality crews. The Ministry of Defence was extremely worried that it was going to involve substantial cost (equivalent to three *Polaris* submarines) and a drain on skilled manpower and technical resources (thereby interfering with Britain's own nuclear programme) in order to produce a capability that was quite superfluous to requirements. Nor was there much enthusiasm for a German finger on the nuclear button (although German fingers were already close to 'tactical' nuclear weapon buttons through the dual-key system) or suggestions that MLF might develop into a purely European deterrent, which would have superseded any unique British contribution.

Not wishing to offend the Americans, Britain agreed to investigate the feasibility of MLF. It was difficult to denounce the exercise because of certain phrases in the Nassau Agreement; because of the dangers of nuclear cooperation which excluded Britain, either between the United States and Germany or, more ominous still, France and Germany; and because of the danger of being excluded from the contracts to provide the necessary equipment. In December 1963 Britain put forward its own proposals to create a MLF out of existing medium- and intermediate-range missiles and aircraft owned by NATO powers, including Britain's

V-bombers but not *Polaris* missiles. The United States was not impressed, seeing this only as a possible supplement to its own scheme – not an alternative. In December 1964, just after the General Election, the new Labour Government, under pressure from Washington to accede to MLF, came up with a new proposal for an Atlantic Nuclear Force (ANF). This involved most of the existing and planned British nuclear force, an equal amount of American forces and a separate multilateral component. The system would be under an international command, but with national vetoes.

In the event ANF helped to demonstrate the hopeless diplomatic tangle generated by the original American proposals which had received little positive support in Europe. ANF was also unattractive to the non-nuclear countries, but Britain was not interested anyway in pushing the matter. Talks continued in a desultory manner through 1965 until the matter was eventually dropped, ostensibly to encourage East–West discussions on a Non-Proliferation Treaty. The problem of participation in nuclear decision-making was eased by the much simpler device of a consultative mechanism involving the non-nuclear powers within NATO, which became known as the Nuclear Planning Group. This reflected a sensible recognition that the problem was political rather than operational in nature; the need was to reassure allies that decisions critical to their destiny were not wholly beyond their influence. A move in this direction had been made with the Athens Guidelines on consultation before nuclear use, agreed in 1962, and now the Nuclear Planning Group would bring a number of the non-nuclear powers into all stages of peacetime nuclear decision-making.

INDEPENDENCE

If the Labour Party had not won the General Election of October 1964, British strategic thought might well have followed a more Gaullist line. The French argued that, in an age of effective nuclear parity, the Americans could not be expected to risk suicide to defend Europe. Therefore NATO was based on an illusion which the Europeans would do well to recognise. They also claimed that a small nuclear force could operate by itself as an effective deterrent to Soviet aggression because of the greater likelihood that a country would use nuclear weapons in self-defence rather than in defence of others, and also because of 'proportionality'. This concept accepted that the European nuclear forces could do less damage to the Soviet Union than American forces, but argued that they could still exact a sufficient price – 'tearing off an arm' as General De Gaulle put it – for the more limited prize the smaller European countries offered.

At a time when much French diplomacy was based on constant repetition of the twin themes of the incredibility of the US nuclear guarantee and the credibility of small national nuclear forces, it was not surprising that they were echoed in Britain. Sections of the Conservative Party, still infuriated with the Americans for their lack of support over Suez and convinced that the real point of nuclear power was to create added leverage in international affairs, were sympathetic to the Gaullist nostrums. In a circumspect manner, they were reflected in the 1964 Defence White Paper, which noted the

> fact that if there were no power in Europe capable of inflicting unacceptable damage on a potential enemy he might be tempted – if not now then perhaps at some time in the future – to attack in the mistaken belief that the United States would not act unless America herself were attacked. The V-bombers by themselves are, and the *Polaris* submarines will be, capable of inflicting greater damage than any potential aggressor would consider acceptable.'

By assuming that any impression that the United States 'would not act' would be 'mistaken', the White Paper was able to neglect the difficult problem of what would happen if the impression was quite correct. Britain could only act alone if it retained sufficient American good-will to maintain the British force or else was able to act before any American ill-will had come to impair its long-term operational effectiveness, through the denial of spare parts or special materials. Nor was it easy to envisage scenarios in which the sort of reasoning which had led the Americans to hold back on its nuclear guarantee would not result in similar caution in Britain.

This became the gravamen of the Labour Party's critique of Conservative policy. Influenced by current American policy rather than French, Labour took a robust 'anti-Nassau' line in its

1964 manifesto. The agreement was described as adding 'nothing to the deterrent strength of the Western Alliance' and deserving of 'renegotiation'. Rather than 'endless duplication of strategic nuclear weapons' the stress should be on conventional forces.

It became clear after the election that Labour's displeasure was not with the deal reached at Nassau (which was soon recognised to be remarkably favourable to Britain) but the fact that the Conservatives chose to present it as something which preserved the 'independence' of the British deterrent. As Prime Minister, Harold Wilson argued that the extent of the reliance on American technology, materials and equipment meant that 'independence' was purely pretence. The government renounced all 'suggestion of a "go-it-alone" British nuclear war against the Soviet Union', mocking the idea of a 'nuclear Suez' or acting as a 'trigger for the US deterrent'.[2]

The ANF was presented as fulfilment of the pledge to 're-negotiate' the Nassau agreement, though it was mainly designed with reference to the unacceptable MLF. However, even in the ANF proposal Harold Wilson made it clear that 'there will not be any system of locks which interferes with our right of communication with a submarine or our right to withdraw the submarine'.[3] This was not dissimilar from Macmillan's 'supreme national interests' clause in the Nassau Agreement.

The collapse of the ANF and MLF schemes saved Britain concern over the burden of implementing them, and left it as the main European nuclear power (though France was now coming up behind) rather than only a component part of a more broadly based European effort. The theme of 'independence' was now to be played down, and the force wholly committed to NATO for as long as the alliance survived. But the problem remained as before: identifying a distinctive contribution that a small, European nuclear power might make to a NATO strategy when the dominant alliance power had sufficient capability to perform all necessary nuclear missions.

CONTRIBUTION TO NATO

The British V-bombers had been formally assigned to NATO in 1963 and came to be targeted with American forces at the Strategic Air Command headquarters at Omaha, forming part of a Single Integrated Operation Plan (SIOP). Britain's nuclear force was, and still is, described as a contribution to NATO's strategic nuclear deterrent. Yet this was at a time when, admittedly to the loud protests of America's allies, NATO was reducing the role of this deterrent in its plans, preparing to deal with less-than-mortal threats to the very existence of Western civilisation by non-nuclear means.

Moreover, it was not self-evident that NATO needed Britain's strategic force. At its peak of 180 aircraft, which it only reached in 1961, the V-bomber force of *Victors*, *Valiants* and *Vulcans*, because of its proximity to the Warsaw Pact, had certain advantages over the American Strategic Air Command and had sufficient flexibility to pick out enemy targets of compelling local interest. It would have played a prominent part in the 'first wave' of a Western nuclear attack on the Soviet Union. The United States was now building a force of 656 SLBMs on 41 *Polaris* submarines as well as over 1000 intercontinental ballistic missiles (ICBMs). Britain planned five submarines, later cut back to four with 64 SLBMs in total. Its planned missile force was equivalent to less than 4 per cent of that planned by the United States. Moreover, Britain only enjoyed a measure of flexibility at a long range while the V-bombers still had life in them. The *Polaris* SLBMs could attack only a narrow range of targets all of which were more than adequately covered by American forces (although those responsible for the SIOP at Omaha could always think of some extra tasks for the British force).

The idea of a 'contribution' to the NATO deterrent first slipped into Defence White Papers in 1956. In that year the contribution was to be 'substantial – commensurate with our standing as a world power'. Next year, compared with the United States, Britain's contribution was only going to be 'modest', but by 1958 it had become 'increasingly significant'. Thereafter, when mentioned, it was the source of the contribution rather than its magnitude that was stressed. The fact that this was a European force meant that it was more likely to be responsive to European interests; an extra centre of nuclear decision added uncertainty to Soviet calculations. Denis Healey is quoted by his biographers explaining the 'strategic reason' why the incoming Labour Government decided in 1964 to continue the Polaris programme: 'if you are inside an alliance you increase the deterrent to the other side enormously if there is more than one centre of decision for the first use of nuclear weapons'.[4]

We will discuss the adequacy of this approach later in the book, for it soon became established as the best available rationale for the nuclear force (see Chapter 12). For the moment it is worth noting that the deterrent effect of separate decision centres relied first on accepting limits to the consultative mechanisms and joint targeting plans that were supposed to ensure that allies acted in harmony in a crisis, and second on there being a distinct possibility that circumstances might arise in which Britain would wish to initiate the use of nuclear weapons while the United States was holding back (or at least the Russians would be impressed by this possibility when assuring themselves that there was a good possibility that the Americans would be holding back). This, in turn, siggests an element of doubt over the quality of the US nuclear guarantee.

A prolonged discussion of the consequences of separate decision centres soon makes it apparent that they could lead either to provoking a nuclear war against American wishes, or else attempting to create a sanctuary for Britain as an East–West conflict was escalating. Speculation as to either possibility raises questions as to Britain's loyalty and responsibility to the alliance.

Similarly it seemed tactful not to make plans with the proposition that the declining credibility of the US nuclear guarantee made a European deterrent vital. The French have not felt so inhibited in using doubts on the American commitment to justify its 'force de frappe'. France followed the logic of the position in 1966 to the extent of withdrawing from NATO's Integrated Military Command, though not from the alliance itself, preferring to rely on its own devices.

Britain was unable to accept the conclusion of this chain of reasoning, which would have involved the end of NATO and American disengagement from Europe. It therefore felt obliged to reject the premise. That the growth of Soviet nuclear capabilities had introduced a major element of uncertainty over the quality of the US nuclear guarantee to Europe could not be denied. However, deterrence is in the eyes of the beholder. The US nuclear arsenal played an important stabilising role so long as the Soviet leaders considered that there was a chance of it being activated in the event of war. As all the alternatives to NATO and the US nuclear guarantee seemed much worse, the course of wisdom was to overcome natural scepticism and affirm confidence in the American commitment. In this way, the proper refusal to countenance the collapse of the alliance deprived Britain of one of the most effective public arguments in favour of an independent force. American disengagement was cited only as a hypothetical possibility for which it was useful to be prepared, but not as a virtual certainty.

THE SEARCH FOR A ROLE

The only reason for maintaining national control over its nuclear force was if circumstances could be contemplated in which Britain would wish to act independently. As Macmillan put it after Nassau,

> there may be conditions, there must be areas, in which the interests of some countries may seem to them more vital than they seem to others. It is right and salutory that a British Government, whatever may be the particular dispute, should be in a position to make their own decision without fear of nuclear blackmail.[5]

At the time of this statement Britain was still a country with a wide range of military responsibilities outside NATO. It was difficult to demonstrate how any military operations outside of Europe could be usefully supported by nuclear power, because of the danger of getting into a nuclear war with the Soviet Union on matters of peripheral interests or of the ignominy that would attach to any nation inflicting devastation on undefended people in the Third World. However, it was possible to argue that nuclear weapons might provide cover against Soviet nuclear threats directed against Britain to persuade it to desist from legitimate conventional operations.

It was just about possible to conceive of offering a British guarantee to Commonwealth countries threatened by a neighbouring power, although it would be difficult to be taken seriously if the neighbour was the Soviet Union. Although Harold Wilson normally derided ideas such as this, he did toy publicly at one point with the idea of providing a nuclear guarantee to India against China, which exploded its first atomic bomb as Labour came to power in October 1964. The Labour Government's first Defence White Paper remarked on the 'shadow' cast by this explosion in an 'area where we have Commonwealth and treaty responsibilities to assist our friends'. It noted that: 'Our nuclear policy must help to provide some reassurance to non-nuclear powers'.[6] Nuclear-armed V-bombers were for a time located in Singapore, and Wilson pointedly excluded part of this force from the ANF proposal.

Whatever the virtues of this idea in principle it could not get very far in practice simply because nuclear weapons could not compensate for weaknesses in Britain's position, including the limited conventional assistance it could bring to a beleaguered friend and the small size of the nuclear force which meant that there was insufficient 'deterrence' available both for Europe and all Commonwealth countries in Asia. Moreover, the idea was not taken very seriously by the Indians themselves.

As it became accepted that it would be folly to emply nuclear weapons until all other alternatives had been exhausted in any given conflict, it was unlikely that nuclear threats were going to be invoked outside of Europe unless disputes were incapable of solution by conventional means. In 1967, economic pressures forced Britain to accept that it could no longer sustain a significant military presence East of Suez. Thereafter there was to be a contraction of the British military effort to the NATO area. If Britain was no longer to engage in prolonged conventional operations outside of Europe, the possibilities of any nuclear operations became minimal. If there was a rationale for independent forces, more than ever before it had to be found in the European theatre.

In Europe, too, there were major problems in identifying circumstances in which British interests would diverge from those of others, without putting oneself in the Gaullist camp, by putting limits on loyalty to the Alliance and its declared doctrines and procedures, or dwelling unduly on the quality of the US nuclear guarantee.

During the 1960s this problem was intensified. The growth of the US nuclear capabilities and the move towards a flexible response strategy in which nuclear strikes were only for use high up the escalation ladder made it difficult to identify ways in which the British force provided a serious complement to that of the United States. The collapse of various schemes for multilateral and multinational forces accentuated the problem of identifying any distinctive British role. In the end, the best rationale that could be managed was one which pointed to the uncertainty that might exist in the Soviet mind over whether the British nuclear force would be activated in unison with that of the United States. Awkward speculations on the possible grounds that might justify such uncertainty were discouraged. The response to the dilemma of constructing a strategic rationale that was plausible but did not undermine the fundamental articles of faith of NATO came to be an embarrassed and resolute silence.

4 The Labour Government and Nuclear Weapons 1964–70

The Labour Party won the October 1964 general election after a campaign during which the Conservative Party had suggested that the future of the nuclear deterrent was at stake. Yet the *Polaris* programme survived the new Government, with the only slight concession to the anti-nuclear lobby being the cut of the planned force from five to four boats.

The Labour Party had refused to be drawn on the nuclear issue during the election campaign. Hugh Gaitskell as leader had fought hard with the unilateral disarmers within the party. But following his death, and with the growing political isolation of the disarmers themselves, the party managers had found it possible to calm passions. They had no desire to see the controversy return. In this, they were helped by a general sense that the world was no longer hurtling to nuclear disaster. The relative optimism was the result of the firm handling of the Cuban Missile Crisis, succeeded by the first signs of detente – the 'hot line' agreement and the Partial Test Ban Treaty.

On taking office the new Government was therefore not determined to cancel *Polaris*; but the shift had not gone so far as to become a commitment to go ahead with the programme come what may. When Denis Healey began work as Defence Secretary his first questions on *Polaris* were quite practical. What was the state of the programme? Could it be speeded up? Could it be cancelled? It soon became clear to Healey and Harold Wilson that the *Polaris* deal had been a good one and, with Foreign Secretary Patrick Gordon Walker, they decided in principle to endorse it.

31

In the middle of November a briefing was arranged for virtually the whole Cabinet to indicate the cost-effectiveness of *Polaris*. The Ministers were told that the budgetary burden of the new system would be moderate, that the hardware being purchased would last a whole generation and not be overtaken by technological advances, that the progress to date indicated that the building programme would be completed on time and at cost. To bring home the fact that, in spite of being small compared with the super-powers' strategic force, the British *Polaris* fleet would still be able to pack a punch, the Ministers were told that missiles from three of the submarines would be able to destroy 15 to 24 cities and up to 25 million of the Soviet population.

A week later (21–22 November) the Cabinet held a defence conference at Chequers. According to Harold Wilson the decision to proceed with *Polaris* was not 'under review'. Denis Healey's biographers, however, report a 'tremendous argument' at this conference, with George Wigg and Lord Chalfont against continuation of the programme, only for their arguments to be demolished by Healey and the decision to go against them taken on the Sunday.[1]

It has been suggested that one good reason for not abandoning *Polaris* was the exorbitant cancellation costs written into the contracts. In fact the Treasury had been holding back on authorising new expenditure during 1964 until the election was over. By the time Labour came to power, £40 million had been spent and another £270 million had been committed on all aspects of the programme. The net cost of foreclosing would have been £35–40 million (net because a number of the ordered items could be put to other uses). This was not prohibitive.

The low cost of *Polaris* was an extremely influential factor. Even while the force was being built its cost barely reached 5 per cent of the budget and it was known that operating costs, once constructed, would be under 2 per cent. The main reason for this was the enormous American subsidy in making available information relating to the design of the submarines and warheads for *Polaris* and accepting only a limited contribution to the development costs of the missile, which would have been an additional 12 per cent on the production cost on a *pro-rata* base. This matter was overlooked at Nassau, leading the British to assume that they would not be expected to pay development costs. However, as the British were opting for a version of the missile (A-3) still under development, the Americans requested some contributions to these costs. Harold Macmillan noted at the time: 'I have refused to make an open-ended contribution to an unknown bill for Research and Development. But I have offered, in lieu, to add five per cent to the retail cost . . . not a bad bargain.'[2] By going directly to President Kennedy, over the head of Secretary of Defence Robert McNamara, Macmillan got his way. The saving in fact was less than it might have been because the production price turned out to be so low. The capital cost for purchasing the missiles had been estimated originally to be £92.9 million. Allowing for inflation, it came out at 42 per cent less, at £53 million. Even the submarines were comparatively inexpensive and did not stray too far from the original estimate of £140.3 million, coming out at 6 per cent higher in real terms at £162 million. In consequence the whole programme cost 13 per cent less than anticipated (although the original estimates were very much guesswork)[3] as well as arriving on schedule, a most unusual phenomenon.

THE FIFTH SUBMARINE

In January 1965 the Government confirmed the decision to go ahead with the programme. There was, however, to be one change. Instead of five boats there were to be four. As we shall see, this had important consequences and in retrospect appears as an example of false economy. However to keep the matter in perspective two points should be noted.

First, the fifth boat had been in doubt during the previous Government. At Nassau four boats were agreed and there was an option on a fifth, to be decided upon by the end of 1963. During 1963 the feeling among ministers moved from seeing the fifth boat as an integral part of the programme to seeing it as something less essential. The concern was that it would extend – over 1968–71 – the period when the defence budget would be feeling the burden of the capital costs of the nuclear programme. This would be a period when other Air Force and Army programmes would also be peaking. Eventually, the Defence Minister, Peter Thorneycroft, decided that the vagaries of defence planning, a slippage here and a cancellation there, would mean that the money could be found. This was accepted by the Overseas Policy and Defence Committee of the Cabinet in March 1964.

From then until October little was done on the extra boat – no more than long lead-time items were ordered. The cancellation only cost £1 million. When Denis Healey began work at the Ministry of Defence one of the first studies he ordered was on whether a three-, four- or five-boat force would suffice for a minimum deterrent. Some, for example in the Treasury, argued for three boats, but four was a satisfactory compromise – the fifth seemed surplus to requirements.

The second point is that the Royal Navy did not take issue with this decision. There was relief that the whole programme was not to be cancelled and some feeling that, because of the difficulty of finding skilled civilian and military manpower, there was something to be said for making do with one less boat. In the major debate on the future of the Royal Navy that took place in the 1960s, the Admirals seemed content with their minimum SLBM force and more worried about the rest of their fleet.

Nevertheless, the decision to cancel the fifth boat has turned out to be false economy. The reason for this is found in the operating pattern of the submarines, which was established when the first one became operational in June 1968 and has been adhered to since. Each of the four boats – *Resolution, Renown, Repulse* and *Revenge* – has two crews of 14 officers and 129 ratings. (It had been originally planned to have 131 crew but it was found that extra personnel, including a doctor, were needed.) Each crew expects to spend 12 weeks with the boat before it is relieved by the alternate crew. Of this 12 weeks some 4 weeks is spent in routine trials and maintenance with the other 8 actually spent submerged on station or *en route* to the patrol area. Consequently, two boats should be on patrol for around 8 months of the year, and three boats for the other 4 months. However, each of the boats must be withdrawn for long re-fits to the dockyard at Rosyth. During these long re-fits the safety system is checked, the nuclear reactor core replaced and a certain amount of stabilising work undertaken. The replacement of the reactor core involves cutting through the hull and the reactor vessel before taking out the old core, replacing it and welding the whole thing together again.

It was assumed initially that the whole re-fit operation would take 15 months, of which 12 would be spent in the actual re-fit, 1 in preparing for the re-fit and 2 in working up afterwards to an operational capability. But, in making this estimate the planners could draw upon almost no practical experience: in 1963 even the

American ballistic-missile-carrying submarines had yet to go through their first re-fits. Also, this is the aspect of the *Polaris* operation that is the least under systematic control, and more dependent on the vicissitudes of dockyard life. In the event the re-fits have proved more complicated than originally envisaged. there has always been something extra to do and the total period off duty has become 18–20 months.

The time between re-fits for each boat is some $3\frac{1}{2}$ years. (The first boat, *Resolution*, began its first re-fit a bit early, but this was so as to establish a re-fit cycle for the whole fleet.) The main determinant of the re-fit cycle is not the longevity of the reactor core but the need to check the state of the submarine's diving system. The development of a new reactor core, which could last for $5\frac{1}{2}$ rather than $3\frac{1}{2}$ years, was of only limited benefit when it came to the re-scheduling of re-fits.

What all this means is that for about half of each year only one boat is on station. It is the case that given warning time of more than a day an extra boat can usually be got out to sea or asked to extend its patrol (supplies for another month are kept on board). Furthermore, missiles could be fired from a boat at base in Faslane on the Clyde in an emergency at some 25 minutes' notice, but Faslane would be a prime target for any surprise attack. Boats not on patrol cannot be considered available for retaliation against a surprise 'bolt from the blue', but otherwise they might well be made available to reinforce the deterrent during a crisis. Given the relative invulnerability of submarines one boat on patrol still constitutes a formidable force. Nevertheless, it is necessary to accept a modest danger of this boat being found and destroyed by an enemy. This threat to the survival of the force is reduced enormously (by much more than half) when an extra boat is available. The major problem with a four-boat force is that it is the absolute minimum. With only three boats, a prolonged period without any on station would be unavoidable and the force would lose credibility as a deterrent. The decision to cut the fifth boat left the credibility of the whole force vulnerable to the loss, through accident or old age, of one of the remaining four.

The other consequence of the decision to cancel the fifth boat was that it reduced the total number of missiles from 80 to 64 (each boat carries 16). The *Polaris* missiles have a range of 2500 nautical miles (2800 statute miles). After some consideration had been given to the possibility of taking the cheaper and proven A-2

Polaris with a single warhead, it was decided to follow the American line of development with its A-3 *Polaris* and fit a warhead capable of dividing into three, each with a yield of some 200 kilotons. These warheads are released in a shotgun effect and can be distributed around a target, with some 10 miles between each explosion. They lack the accuracy and wider separation of the more advanced multiple independently targeted re-entry vehicles (MIRVs). When it is remembered that the bomb that destroyed Hiroshima had a yield of some 15 kilotons, it can be seen that a power of awesome destructive potential resides in each re-entry vehicle. Calculations on the probable casualties from individual detonations, which can become quite macabre, depend on the nature of the target and a variety of uncertainties. As a rough guide one could assume that each *Polaris* missile hitting a city centre could kill, directly or indirectly, some one-quarter of a million people, with another half a million injuries, and perhaps many more. The damage to the Soviet Union could be maximised by targeting strategies which attacked vulnerable points in its economy, such as oil refineries or nuclear power stations, or even farmland at harvest time. It should not therefore be thought that, because of the comparative size of the arsenals of the superpowers, the missiles contained in even one *Polaris* submarine do not present a serious nuclear threat. They could inflict a catastrophe of immense proportions on the Soviet people.

The potential limiting factor to the effectiveness of the nuclear force has not been the magnitude of the destructive yield nor serious advances in anti-submarine warfare (ASW), but the prospect of the Soviet Union mounting an efficient ballistic missile defence. Soviet air defences were one reason for the decline in confidence in aircraft as reliable delivery vehicles.

There was a natural fear that a similar fate could befall a missile force. The defensive problem posed by missiles is much greater than that posed by bombers. The speed of a ballistic missile provides little time for detection, identification, tracking and interception. Designing a missile to intercept another missile is the least of the difficulties. The trick is to ensure that it gets the necessary information on an incoming missile in time. In the 1960s, considerable resources were devoted to the design of an efficient ballistic missile defence both in the Soviet Union and the United States. Senior officials in the Pentagon were sceptical as to whether an effective defence was feasible. Available designs were at the limits of technology, would be extremely expensive to introduce, yet could probably be degraded by relatively simple improvements in the offence, involving additional targets for the defence, some of which could be decoys or other devices to fool radars, some of which could be multiple warheads from individual missiles.

In the mid-1960s, intelligence information made it clear that the Soviet Union was busily engaged in constructing an antiballistic missile (ABM) system around Moscow, code-named *Galosh*. At the time NATO estimates assumed that this system would be completed by the late 1960s and would then be expanded to protect most major Soviet cities. In November 1966 the United States publicly revealed what was known about *Galosh*. One response also announced was to move forward with a new SLBM – *Poseidon*. What did not become public until a year later was that this missile was to have multiple independently targetable re-entry vehicles. The new acronym of MIRV had yet to become familiar in strategic debate.

POSEIDON

In September 1967 the United States announced that it was going to deploy an ABM system, but only to protect cities against small attacks from China. The message from this move was that while ABMs might be of little use against major attacks from a superpower they could neutralise small nuclear powers. In the American, and later the Soviet, case, the small power in question was China but the concept was relevant to Britain and France. Meanwhile, it appeared that the American move to MIRVs, as a means of strengthening the offence in the face of the new defensive challenge, left the British *Polaris* force obsolescent while still in early infancy. *Poseidon* would split up into ten or more warheads, each to be sent to a separate target and each with an explosive yield of some 50 kilotons. As it became operational the Americans would already be preparing a follow-on force. *The Economist* reported gloomily that:

On the assumption that anti-missile technology is now really getting under way, the only safe estimate is that by the mid-1970s Britain's *Polaris* missiles will be capable of inflicting only

marginal damage on the Russians. [By 1975, Britain] will
either have to get something better than *Polaris* missiles or get
out of the independent nuclear business altogether.[4]

Poseidon was by no means a complete surprise to the British. At
the time of the Nassau Agreement, the American Navy had
alerted the Royal Navy to some of the development work in
progress. Article IV of the Polaris Sales Agreement kept open the
possibility of Britain receiving 'future development relating to the
Polaris Weapon System, including all modifications made
thereto'. On a liberal interpretation this could include follow-on
systems such as *Poseidon* (which had only escaped from being
called the *Polaris* C-3 by President Johnson's desire to impress
Congress with new initiatives).[5] The close cooperation in the
missiles area ensured that the Royal Navy was kept *au fait* with the
progress of *Poseidon*. Indeed the Special Projects Office of the US
Navy (dealing with the ballistic missile force) had a clear interest
in promoting the *Poseidon* concept with its counterpart in the
Royal Navy. A British commitment would lower the unit cost of
the missile and so make it more attractive to the US Administration. For its part the Royal Navy had little option but to consider
Poseidon, for whatever its intrinsic merits its deployment by the
United States would effect the development of ancillary equipment, such as fire control systems, and, as the United States ran
down the production of *Polaris* for its own use, financing arrangements for the provision of spare parts. An assessment of the
implications of *Poseidon* was circulating within the Ministry of
Defence in 1966 before the American decision to authorise full
development in November.

Although those responsible for the *Polaris* fleet were enamoured
of the idea of replacement by *Poseidon*, as a means of keeping up
with, and deriving the benefits of, the latest technology, in
practice the American move had come at least 5 years too early.
The Americans were to use *Poseidon* to replace their single-
warhead *Polaris* A-1 and A-2 missiles – not the multiple-warhead
A-3. The Americans did not consider the particular model of
Polaris that Britain owned to be a candidate for replacement. It
was therefore difficult to demonstrate an actual British requirement.

The Government did not take long to decide not to follow the
Americans immediately with *Poseidon*. Harold Wilson told Parlia-

ment of the rejection of this option in an answer to a written question in June 1967.[6] Richard Crossman implies that the matter was not actually discussed at the Overseas Policy and Defence Committee of the Cabinet, mainly because it was not controversial.[7] In fact it did appear before the Committee but only in the context of a description of general equipment plans.

The Labour Government accepted *Polaris*, against the wishes of many backbenchers, on the ground of its impressive cost-effectiveness. It was unlikely to be over-impressed by a proposal to replace the missiles at some expense – in the region of £150 million – so soon after they had become operational, especially when this would provoke major dissent in the Party. Furthermore, as the Government was engaged in yet another futile attempt to join the European Community, a rejection of *Poseidon* could be presented to the doubting French as evidence that the leopard had, at last, changed its spots. Harold Wilson records in his memoirs informing President de Gaulle of this 'Nassau in reverse' in order to persuade him that Britain was reducing its dependence on the United States.[8]

The difficulty with *Poseidon* was with the warheads. The existing submarines could be modified, at some expense, to take the new missile. Apart from the ability to carry a much more sophisticated warhead, and some benefits in range, *Poseidon* had few advantages over *Polaris* that were worth the expenditure of a few million pounds per copy. As for the warhead, Britain would have to make that itself anyway. It was not that Britain could not have made a MIRVed warhead. The research teams at Aldermaston understood the technology. In fact Britain had helped the American programme by advising on areas of this technology where it had the lead. But there was no need for high missile accuracy. The only interest was in the penetration of ABMs, for which a more sophisticated version of the existing type of warhead could well be sufficient. Another problem was that full MIRV development would require a number of underground nuclear tests. This could be politically damaging, drawing the Labour Party's attention to exertions in an area where it expected the Government to be running down the national effort.

Instead of procuring *Poseidon*, it was decided to redirect the warhead research programme already under way at Aldermaston to an investigation of the possibility of a new warhead for *Polaris* which would improve its capability to penetrate Soviet defences through greater accuracy, warhead hardening and decoys. This programme was criticised by some who would have preferred to see research into nuclear energy devoted much more to civil than military applications. Continued warhead research at Aldermaston was eventually authorised. It would keep options open for the future should the Soviet ABM problem become acute. As important a consideration was that if Britain fell behind in nuclear research then its ability to enter into or sustain reciprocal, cooperative relationships with other nations would be impaired. This was relevant both to the continuation of the existing close ties with the United States, and possible links in the future with France. One of the claims made by Harold Wilson in the attempt to gain admission to the European Community was that Britain could offer Europe advanced technological capabilities.

5 *Chevaline*

In the decade following Nassau the strategic environment changed. The Soviet Union caught up, at least quantitatively, in strategic arms with the United States. Defensive technology failed to live up to its early promise but offensive technology advanced on all fronts, leading to missiles of greater range, multiplying the warhead each could carry, allowing for targets to be reached through subtle in-flight manoeuvres and attacked with high accuracy. Moreover, the political environment had changed. The United States lost self-confidence and esteem in Vietnam. Britain's relative decline, already evident in 1962, proceeded apace. While its relationship with the United States retained a number of distinctive features unlikely to be copied by others, it was patently no longer the leading European power. Furthermore by 1972 it was preparing at last to join the European Community, thus accepting that relations with its neighbours were in the future to be more 'special' than those with its old ally across the Atlantic.

It is not surprising that these changes influenced Anglo-American nuclear cooperation. What is remarkable is how limited were the effects. There is little doubt that the American and British nuclear weapons establishments found it useful to talk to each other. The Americans could note the cheaper, and often quite ingenious, solutions the British had been forced to find to common problems. The British were able to pick up some of the fruits of the immense effort that supported the American strategic arsenal.

However, in the second half of the 1960s two problems had begun to appear in the relationship. When technical exchanges had been first permitted there was a great burst of activity, with both sides curious to know how the other had dealt with the problems of developing and producing nuclear weapons over the

1950s. Then, as both were working in parallel on *Polaris* submarines and missiles there was much to discuss. However, once
the major issues in these programmes had been sorted out there
was less to talk about.

From 1966 on a diminution of interest on the American side
could be detected. Admiral Hyman Rickover, in charge of the
development of America's sea-based deterrent, wanted to limit
the information exchanges. He was supported by those sceptical
of the intention of the Labour Government in Britain in this area.
This was not only because this Government's commitment to the
nuclear deterrent was doubted, but also because of concern that it
was prepared to pass on sensitive information to other European
governments if this would ease entry into the European Community. These suspicions grew when Britain joined West Germany
and Holland in a project to enrich uranium through a centrifuge
project for civil nuclear purposes. It was claimed in the United
States that the British contribution to this was derived from a joint
US–UK project of the mid-1950s. Britain claimed that the new
technology was far removed from the old technology. This argument came at a time when the 1959 amendments to the 1958 acts
were being renegotiated. Agreement was reached in 1969 with
difficulty, after an American attempt to tie Britain down on how
any materials and information it obtained from the United States
were to be used. The review period was cut from 10 to 5 years.
(There have been no comparable problems in the subsequent
reviews, the last of which was concluded satisfactorily in December 1979.)

The suspicion of trends in British policy was underlined by the
build-up to the 1970 campaign. Discussion of the 'independent'
deterrent was conspicuous for its absence, but there seemed to be
a strong pro-European consensus. Edward Heath, leader of the
opposition, was known to be particularly anxious to secure entry
into the Community and was thought willing to contemplate
nuclear collaboration as part of the Community's future development. In 1967 he spoke of the possibility of a European defence
system, including 'a nuclear force based on the existing British
and French forces which could be held in trusteeship for Europe
as a whole'.[1] Less quoted, however, is the previous passage in this
speech which suggested that any move of this sort would require
the creation of a united political authority for Western Europe.

When Heath won the election in June 1970 and the Conservatives came to power the situation soon improved. It became clear that the new Government was interested in improving the quality of the nuclear force and that this would be done through cooperation with the United States rather than France. There were some discussions with the French on possible collaboration, but the problem caused by France's absence from NATO's consultative councils, the inhibitions on information exchange resulting from past Anglo-American agreements and the differences in timetables and approach meant that the matter had to be relegated to the long term.[2] When, in the early 1970s, it was suggested that the French and British navies might like to get together to discuss their common problems in managing ballistic missile submarines the variety of limitations on what was permissible to discuss eventually left little on the agenda but the dietary needs of submariners (this episode was known in the MOD as the 'cornflake saga').

On the American side, the new Republican Administration of Richard Nixon, as advised by Dr Henry Kissinger, was much more philosophically committed to the idea of encouraging allies to build up their own military capabilities rather than rely excessively on American intervention in a crisis.

THE CONSERVATIVES AND *POLARIS*

As the new Conservative Government began to examine the state of the *Polaris* force the situation appeared largely satisfactory. The nuclear decision of the previous Conservative Administration had been implemented, with the only amendent being the cancellation of the fifth submarine. The *Polaris* force had recently taken over the strategic role from the V-bombers.

The position was thus better than might have been hoped in 1962. The programme had been completed on time at a low cost. It was not under immediate threat from new technologies. There were grounds for confidence that anti-submarine warfare techniques were far from the point where the submarines were in serious danger. Meanwhile, the Soviet Union appeared to have developed doubts over the quality of its *Galosh* ABM defence around Moscow. Such concerns as did exist were over the problems of keeping at least one boat on station.

In June 1970, as at the time of the election, the first of the

submarines, *Resolution*, began its long re-fit. It had already become evident that the re-fit was going to be much longer and more
difficult than envisaged. Lord Carrington, the new Secretary of
Defence, considered the possibility of building a fifth submarine,
and purchasing extra missiles from the United States. The Government decided against this. In 1973, the capital cost of a fifth
Polaris submarine, including missiles, warheads and works services, was estimated to be in the order of £90 million, with running
costs at about £8 million a year.[3]

The problem was that this would take 7–8 years, by which time
doubts about the quality of the actual missiles might have grown.
In order to keep extra boats on patrol it was considered assigning
them to operational stations closer to shore. The need to get to a
distant station quickly puts a strain on the hulls and propulsion
machinery. It was hoped that these measures would obviate the
need for any extra boats, while the prospects for qualitative
improvements were re-examined.

The occasion for this review was the successful completion of
the first round of Strategic Arms Limitation Talks (SALT)
between the Soviet Union and the United States. There was
concern in Whitehall that in future SALT discussions the United
States might accept clauses limiting its freedom to transfer whole
weapons systems or relevant technologies to allies. During the
SALT I negotiations the Americans had to be warned off this, at
least as far as offensive weapons were concerned. Their NATO
allies let the matter pass in the ABM Treaty because they had
little interest themselves in the relevant technology. Article IX of
the SALT Treaty limiting ABMs, signed in Moscow in May 1972,
included a restrictive non-transfer clause. Though the Americans
issued a unilateral statement to the effect that Article IX did 'not
set a precedent for whatever provision may be considered' by a
future Treaty on Offensive Arms,[4] the danger remained. A second
cause of anxiety was some of the sentiments expressed during
Senator George McGovern's campaign for the Presidency. Although McGovern was roundly defeated in November 1972 by
Richard Nixon, considered sympathetic to the strategic needs of
allies, it was felt that in 1976 the next President might be less
amenable. (This is an assumption commonly made in Whitehall
about any President and his successor, and is based on the 'devil
you know' principle.)

The ABM Treaty had also clarified the extent of the defensive problem that the British force was going to have to face in the coming years. The problem was not going to be as hopeless as it would have been had future Soviet ABM deployments been enthusiastic and uninhibited. Nevertheless, a limited problem remained, and officials began to consider whether, in the light of the *Galosh* system protecting Moscow and the apparent Soviet determination to improve it, Britain would be able to preserve the existing range of targeting options for its nuclear force.

During 1972 studies were conducted between the US Navy and the Royal Navy on the possibility of converting the British fleet to take the *Poseidon* SLBM. The studies resulted in a proposal to go ahead with a conversion. It was based on a preference for keeping up with Americans in the line of its force development, rather than staying with a missile that had been superseded by a newer and better model, and a belief that the cost would not be exorbitant. This was estimated to be in the region of £250 million, in line with estimates of 5 years previously when the Labour Government had considered *Poseidon*.

There were other studies, organised at the highest level in Washington and London, to consider how best to improve the quality of the British force. The studies did not confine themselves to the *Poseidon* option but considered others derived from the warhead research that had been set in motion at Aldermaston in 1967.

When Prime Minister Edward Heath visited Washington in early 1973, he raised the question of *Poseidon* in an exploratory manner. Not only was Heath reassured on the renewal of the agreement, but he found the Administration quite enthusiastic over assisting Britain to enhance the quality of its strategic forces. Nevertheless, by the middle of the year the British Government had decided against *Poseidon* and in favour of an alternative approach.

If a recent interview by Dr Kissinger is to be believed, this disappointed the Americans:

> When . . . I was in Office I urged my British counterparts to opt for the most modern system which we would have been willing to give them, and to urge our Government to give the British our most modern system. For a variety of reasons the British thought this was too expensive at the time, and chose a somewhat less than the most modern system.[5]

This was not the impression that the British gained at the time. Kissinger did not refuse Britain *Poseidon,* but nor did he press it upon them. Instead, he spoke at some length on the obstacles to this purchase. SALT, he explained, was the least of these. The arms-control negotiations were beginning to move into qualitative restraints on offensive arms, and the acquisition by Britain of the MIRVed *Poseidon* would cause some difficulties, but none that were insuperable. The problem, he suggested, was more that Congress was in an awkward mood on this sort of issue and was likely to refuse to countenance the transfer of this particularly advanced piece of American technology.

POSEIDON OR *CHEVALINE*

The British decision was based on an assessment of both strategic and political factors. The strategic assessment revolved around the Soviet ABM system.

Contrary to expectations during the mid-1960s, the Soviet Union had not introduced nationwide ballistic missile defence. The project had been suspended after only 64 ABM launchers had been deployed in the *Galosh* network around Moscow – coincidentally the same number as the British *Polaris* force. In May 1972 the SALT I Treaty limited the two super-powers to 200 ABM launchers each.

This kept the problem for a small offensive force within manageable limits but by no means removed it altogether. The British planners were concerned that if nuclear retaliation became necessary, and only one submarine was spared after a Soviet surprise attack, the 16 missiles in this submarine would be unable to attack Moscow. Intelligence information suggested that important improvements to the radar associated with *Galosh* were about to be introduced. The calculation is somewhat more complicated than noting that 64 ABMs should be able to manage 16 targets (the *Polaris* A-3 warhead could not separate early enough into three to make it 48 targets). The reliability of the ABMs, and the number required to attack each incoming missile, as well as the reliability of the *Polaris* SLBMs themselves, have to be taken into account. The area of uncertainty is enormous, but assuming the worst in each variable, a significant probability emerges of no missile reaching its target. Certainly, the extent to which the

attack would have to be dedicated to Moscow would leave no
spare capacity for other targets. The margins were such that if the
fifth submarine had been available, ensuring two boats on station
at all times, there could have been much more confidence with
regard to mounting an attack on Moscow, as well as other cities.

In 1973, it might have been assumed that the Soviet Union
would take up the full quota of 100 missiles permitted by the ABM
Treaty for the area defence around Moscow, and also take up the
allowance of another 100 missiles for another ABM site. This
second allowance was withdrawn in 1974 by an amendment to the
original Treaty, by which time it had also become clear that there
was little Soviet interest in completing the Moscow defences.

The *Galosh* system protects more than Moscow itself, perhaps
all the territory within a 200-mile radius of the city. In 1973 it was
noted that the 16 most populous cities outside the Moscow area
contained some 15 million people, as well as 'many high value
targets, such as major dams and waterways, major oil refineries,
major naval shipyards, major iron and steelworks and major
nuclear reactor establishments. Any could be attacked by a single
British submarine patrolling, for example, in the Greenland sea.'[6]
Serious damage could be done to Soviet society while ignoring
Moscow altogether.

The argument in favour of ensuring an ability to attack Moscow is that those ruling the Soviet Union value Moscow far above
any other city, not only because that is where they reside but also
because in a society as centralised as that of the Soviet Union the
disruption caused by the loss of Moscow would far outweigh the
loss of any other centre.

There were two main options for ensuring an ability to penetrate the Moscow defences. The first was the *Poseidon* SLBM, a
new missile with a MIRVed front-end, dividing up into 10–14
warheads, each of some 50 kilotons yield. The other option was to
fit a new front-end to *Polaris.*

The alternative approach to *Poseidon* had also begun life as an
American concept in the first half of the 1960s. The development
of SLBMs was moving from the single-warhead *Polaris* A-1 and
A-2 to the shotgun effect of the triple-headed *Polaris* A-3 (the
design followed by the British). It eventually moved on the
MIRVed *Poseidon* C-4. However, as an alternative to *Poseidon* an
approach known as *Antelope 1* was studied, which concentrated
less on the capacity to hit many targets with some accuracy, to be

found in the full MIRV, and more on the ability to penetrate ABMs.

The *Antelope* approach was, as was the MIRV, intended to provide extra targets for the defensive missiles by extra warheads, including decoys, and also, by adjusting either the trajectory of individual missiles or the flight of the nose cones, to allow them to arrive at about the same time to swamp the defence. Normally, the intervals between firing missiles from a submarine, necessitated by the destabilising consequences of the rush of water filling the spaces vacated if too many missiles are launched too quickly, means that the defence has time to adjust to each incoming missile.

When in 1967 the nuclear weapons research establishment at Aldermaston was asked to consider improvements that might be necessary to sustain *Polaris* through the second half of the submarine fleet's existence, it was natural for the *Antelope* concept to be one of the major options investigated. The Aldermaston scientists were told to undertake serious studies but no more. This they did for the next 5 years, engaging in some discussions with their counterparts in the United States. By 1973, they had decided upon a variation of the *Antelope* approach, now known as *Super-Antelope.*

The concept was refined during 1973, until it went into development under the curious code-name *Chevaline.* There is a belief in the Ministry of Defence that *Chevaline* refers to a species of *Antelope* which is akin to a mountain goat and is supposed to share with the new warhead the ability to move in a variety of directions at high altitudes. However, I have been unable to confirm this in any authoritative encyclopaedia or dictionary. The normal meaning is 'equine' and in French it can have pejorative connotations, for example, in describing the face of an ugly lady or the meat of a bad butcher.

Chevaline was officially described for the first time in 1980 by the Defence Secretary Mr Francis Pym. He spoke of it as:

a very major and complex development of the missile front end, involving also changes to the fire control system. The result will not be a MIRVed system. But it includes advanced penetration aids and the ability to manoeuvre the payload in space.[7]

A few details can be added to this description. In terms of penetrating ABMs the key feature of *Chevaline* is not the number of individual warheads but (i) the ability to change course, angle of re-entry into the atmosphere and the speed of descent so as to confuse the defence; (ii) their early separation before they arrive within range of the defences; (iii) the inclusion in the re-entry package of a number of decoys with the same characteristics as the genuine articles; (iv) hardening to protect the internal electronics from the effects of nuclear explosions in the vicinity. The exact nature of the warhead package is not known.

The configuration most often mentioned is six warheads of 40 kilotons each. However, the origins of this figure lie in some hypothetical calculations undertaken by the International Institute for Strategic Studies (IISS) for the House of Commons Expenditure Committee in early 1973, before the new programme had been approved by the Government (although a warhead with this configuration was discussed during the early Aldermaston studies). It may well involve three warheads as with the A-3, but with the addition of dummies.

In the joint Anglo-American technical assessments of the alternative approaches in 1973, the Americans felt the British lacked ambition in rejecting *Poseidon*, staying with an intermediate technology and so losing the full benefits of MIRVs. They noted the British were extremely worried about expense. Careful cost estimates revealed that the original Navy figure of some £250 million may have been hopelessly optimistic, and though the United States would offer favourable terms the final figure was likely to be over £500 million. Furthermore, the burden to the defence budget would be at its greatest in the late 1970s, when the budget would also be under substantial pressure from the Multi-Role Combat Aircraft (*Tornado*) programme. Figures of the order of £100–£150 million were discussed at the time for *Super-Antelope* although they were recognised to be uncertain estimates. A programme that involves a large amount of new development work and is only to be produced in a limited number of units is extremely vulnerable to cost-escalation. This, in fact, was what happened – to the extent that it is arguable that it would have been less expensive to opt for *Poseidon*.

Another consideration was that if it was desired to follow the

MIRV route it was advisable to wait for the generation after *Poseidon*. In order to gain military endorsement of SALT I in 1972 the Nixon Administration had authorised an acceleration in development of a follow-on to *Poseidon*, then known as the Underwater Long-Range Missile System (ULMS), and now known as *Trident*.

The main arguments for deciding in favour of *Super-Antelope* were political. It had two distinct, if negative, advantages over *Poseidon*: it would not require a major – and public – purchase of missiles from the United States and it would not involve MIRVs. The avoidance of a Nassau-type deal was useful at a time when Britain had, at last, just become a full member of the European Community. However, the main political benefits of *Super-Antelope*'s negative qualities were domestic.

The nuclear programme was no longer a major political issue. There was a quiet and essentially bi-partisan consensus on maintaining the force and not moving to *Poseidon*. This consensus was summed up in a report from the Defence and Foreign Affairs Sub-Committee of the Expenditure Committee that was prepared just as the Government was reaching its own decision. It prescribed the following policy:

> On the limited information available to us we recommend that the Government should maintain the existing *Polaris* fleet and not increase its numbers or MIRV the missiles and should certainly not convert it to *Poseidon*. Anything which can be done within a reasonable cost to make it less vulnerable to enemy ASW [anti-submarine warfare] would, however, have our support.[8]

The Government was happy to follow this line, even to including increasing attention to counter-measures to Soviet ASW activities, such as experiments with various noise-making devices to confuse any Soviet hunter submarines attempting to track *Polaris* submarines.

A move to *Poseidon* would have been politically controversial. We have already noted Kissinger's doubts as to his ability to get a British purchase of *Poseidon* approved in the United States. MIRVs were getting bad publicity as a mischievous development in the arms race. Attention was turning in SALT to means of controlling them. Moreover, the previous Labour Government was on record as opposing *Poseidon*. It would thus have been difficult for the Labour front-bench to avoid a commitment to scrap it if and when it returned to office. If *Poseidon* was adopted and then cancelled, the likelihood was that the deterrent would be abandoned altogether, or at least allowed to die slowly. Without a serious warhead project, the research teams at Aldermaston and elsewhere would disperse, taking with them an expertise that could not easily be recreated. If funds were put instead into less costly, less visible and, in consequence, less controversial *Polaris* improvements then a future Labour Government would be under less political pressure to cancel.

The decision not to opt for *Poseidon* was more definite than the decision in favour of *Chevaline*. *Chevaline* was still a development programme and the relevant decision was to give it some additional focus and momentum. There was little doubt that the programme would be ratified in due course. It was only really confirmed, however, under the Labour Government.

6   The Problem of Replacement

This reasoning turned out to be extremely prescient. At the end of February 1974 the Labour Party won a surprise general election. The new Government was faced with a decision on whether to go ahead with the *Chevaline* programme. There had yet to be a major commitment of expenditure but a decision was needed, certainly before the major review of all defence expenditure promised by the new Government could be completed. Furthermore, the first underground nuclear test for 9 years was planned for May, without which it could not have been ascertained whether *Chevaline* was a feasible project. The test could have been delayed, but at some cost as dates had been booked at the US testing site and new appointments would have taken time to arrange.

The decision was taken, as usual, by a small group – Harold Wilson, Denis Healey, Roy Jenkins, James Callaghan and Roy Mason (Prime Minister, Chancellor and Home, Foreign and Defence Secretaries respectively). The ministers were informed in the first days of the new administration, that a development programme which had been set in motion under the previous Labour Government, had now reached a major point of decision. The objective of this programme, they were told, was no more than to preserve targeting capabilities, now threatened by Soviet ABMs, that had been available to Labour ministers in 1970. They decided to continue with *Chevaline*. In April the Cabinet was informed that a *Polaris* improvement programme was under way at a cost of some £250 million. There was only slight objection.

Among the ministers who were responsible for the decision there was a disposition to keep the nuclear force going for as long as possible. In the Labour Party the main issue was the overall demands made by military expenditure on the national economy rather than any specific features of the defence effort. This issue was to be dealt with by a major defence review, but the actual financial burden caused by the nuclear force was not, as ministers rediscovered, unduly onerous. As a separate issue, the nuclear deterrent had been quiescent for a decade. The important thing was to keep it that way, maintaining the force while not drawing attention to it. There was little interest in innovating in nuclear strategy. Their Conservative predecessors had publicly followed the line established by Labour in 1964 as presenting the nuclear force solely as a contribution to NATO's nuclear deterrent.

The virtues of *Chevaline* did not lie in its strategic rationale but in the fact that it appeared to be the minimum required to keep *Polaris* up to date and postpone a more difficult and visible decision on the matter of wholesale replacement. The aim was to keep a nuclear capability in being. This involved more than maintaining the quality of the *Polaris* fleet. It was also necessary to maintain an adequate design capability for new weapons. It was felt that this would be difficult without, on occasion actually authorising the production of a new warhead. The scientists at Aldermaston and other relevant research establishments had projects related to other types of nuclear weapons, including bombs for strike aircraft, but they had introduced no new strategic weapons since the *Polaris* warhead of the mid-1960s. If *Poseidon* was not to be procured, and the warhead project upon which they had been working since 1967 was to be abandoned with nothing else in the offing until the 1980s, then it would prove difficult to maintain morale at the laboratories and keep together a qualified design team until such time as it could be properly employed. This problem is not unusual in highly specialist areas, in which there are large intervals in between major projects.

Once the design team has been dispersed, the necessary expertise and experience is virtually impossible to regain. Moreover, the responsible scientists were extremely enthusiastic about the opportunity provided by *Chevaline* to develop a difficult warhead of British, rather than American, design.

As might have been expected with an ambitious development programme it came to be delayed and the cost escalated. From an estimated £200 million in 1974 the cost had risen to £450 million at the start of 1976.'

With each cut in the defence budget, common during the first

years of the Labour Government, ministers and some officials
queried tentatively whether *Chevaline* was really indispensable.
The Treasury was particularly dubious. In the summer of 1975,
as the cost escalation became apparent, there was a major review
to see if the programme's continuation would be compatible with
the government's announced intentions to hold down the level of
defence spending. In the middle of 1977, the cost estimates had
risen dramatically to around £800 million, and authorisation was
being requested for the next serious *tranche* of expenditure –
connected with the start of special missile tests in September 1977
at Cape Canaveral in the United States. Ministers seriously
considered aborting the programme. The relevant ministers had
now changed. Fred Mulley and Dr. David Owen had come in as
Defence and Foreign Secretaries, respectively. Mulley was by no
means as enthusiastic about the nuclear force as his predecessor,
Roy Mason, and Owen was quite iconoclastic.

   Chevaline did not survive on its strategic merits. There was some
scepticism over the 'Moscow criterion', that is the belief that it is
absolutely vital for the Soviet capital to be threatened at all times.
Nor was it felt that *Chevaline* represented value for money. It was
recognised that the most sensible course might have been to
purchase *Poseidon* in the first place. Nevertheless, large sums of
money had already been spent and future savings could only be
made by scrapping the programme altogether. It could not be
scaled down. The decision was 'all or nothing'. If it did not
continue there would be no return on the past investment. Lastly,
and perhaps most importantly, it was felt by the few ministers
considering the matter that it would be politically dangerous for a
Labour Government to cancel *Chevaline*. News of a *Polaris Improvement Programme* had reached the public and there were murmur-
ings within and without Whitehall of an incipient *Polaris* replacement issue. Cancellation would be taken as a major turning point
in British nuclear weapons policy, as an indication of being
prepared to wind down the whole force. This was not the Government intention and so the line of least resistance was to let the
programme run its course.

   A major public controversy, in which the left-wing opponents
as well as the right-wing supporters of the nuclear force would
have had their say, might have forced the Government into
premature commitments on nuclear weapons policy. The tradition of secret and bipartisan policy-making, with its emphasis on

continuity, was one reason why the Conservatives chose *Chevaline* in 1973 and why the programme survived in 1977.

In 1980, as *Chevaline* was about to be fitted to the missiles of *Renown*, just entering its long re-fit, the Defence Secretary gave the 'overall estimated cost' of the programme as £1000 million,[2] making it the largest matter in recent years not to have gained a passing mention in the annual defence estimates. Even allowing for inflation, this represents a significant increase over the original estimate. Although details are hard to come by it appears that the new warhead caused less problems than the mechanisms for manoeuvring the front-end in space and guiding it towards the target. About one third of the billion pounds spent on *Chevaline* was spent in the United States, partly on tests, mainly with Lockheed who produce *Polaris*.

REPLACEMENT

In 1974 while deciding to go forward with *Chevaline* the Government made it clear, publicly, that there was no interest in full replacements for *Polaris*, such as *Poseidon*. The existing force was described as a unique and inexpensive contribution to NATO:

> The *Polaris* force, which Britain will continue to make available to the Alliance, provides a unique European contribution to NATO's strategic nuclear capability out of all proportion to the small fraction of our defence budget which it costs to maintain. We shall maintain its effectiveness. We do not intend to move to a new generation of strategic nuclear weapons.[3]

The two key phrases on the future: 'maintain its effectiveness', while renouncing a 'new generation of strategic nuclear weapons' were used, without amendment, for the duration of the Government in response to all enquiries from suspicious backbenchers. Apart from repetition of these phrases, Government ministers were not forthcoming on the question of the nature of the commitments taken to 'maintain the effectiveness of the existing force', or if this might ever require 'a new generation of strategic nuclear weapons'.

There were persistent indications that the Government was taking active steps to maintain *Polaris* – underground nuclear explosions in Nevada and flight tests of missiles. In early 1976 intense suspicion was aroused among Labour backbenchers when it was announced that it had been decided to produce tritium in Britain. This is an isotope of hydrogen used in the fabrication of thermonuclear warheads and has, up to now, been imported from the United States, under the 1958 agreement on nuclear coopera- tion. Unlike other nuclear materials, tritium has only a short half-life (12.3 years) and, therefore, a continual supply is re- quired. It is also difficult to produce, involving cooling lithium rods and then separating the tritium out by a complex extraction process. The official rationale for the 1976 decision was that a new extraction process made the operation less expensive, and that starting production in Britain would save dollars and create extra jobs in the nuclear industry. In addition, the commercial uses of tritium may lead to important export opportunities. It has been suggested that the decision to become self-sufficient in tritium grew out of concern with the anti-proliferation mood in the United States and the possibility of more stringent controls on the transfer of all nuclear fuels. But neither this decision, nor one announced in January 1980 to produce enriched uranium in Britain by means of a gas centrifuge process (largely to ensure a supply of fuel for the power plants of nuclear submarines), will provide complete self-sufficiency. There are still other specialist materials required from the United States. The tritium plant was expected to become operational in 1980.[4] It is not linked to any specific weapons programme. Rather it indicates a continuing interest in sustaining a capability for nuclear weapons produc- tion.

It was not possible for the Labour Government to postpone addressing the long-term questions indefinitely. The problem was not so much one of improvements in Soviet capabilities but of the creeping old age, affecting in different ways the submarines and missiles of the British force.

By 1982 the United States will have withdrawn its final ten *Polaris* submarines from service. At this point, Lockheed, the sole manufacturer, will have no need to keep open its production line for the missiles. This in itself need not cause too many difficulties for Britain could buy stocks of remaining *Polaris* missiles. How- ever, the solid propellants used in the missiles have only a limited shelf-life of a few years.

The Government did take steps to minimise the disruption to

Britain's *Polaris* fleet caused by the phasing out of the American force. It was agreed with the United States that missiles and spare parts needed would continue to be available. Rather than keep open all production lines, some parts could be storable. Mr Mulley, as Defence Secretary, expressed his confidence that 'if kept in the right storage conditions solid fuel propellant is safe and effective for decades'. A new order for 31 *Polaris* missiles was agreed with the United States for delivery in the 1980s. This was in addition to the 102 missiles already delivered. The Ministry also implied that 'mainly as a result of the phasing out of the US *Polaris* force and a consequent full acceptance of costs previously shared' the overall cost of the *Polaris* force could rise by up to 20 per cent.[5]

The real problem was with the submarines. When the submarines were first constructed it has been officially stated that they would have an active life of 20 years. They were brought into service between 1967 and 1969. Original estimates would therefore put their active life coming to an end in the late 1980s. It is generally agreed that this is unduly pessimistic, and that an extra 5 years of active life is quite probable – even longer with luck. Optimists say, with proper care, the boats could last 40 years. The difficulty lies in relying on this; the time taken to construct any replacement ensures that decisions to replace cannot be taken at the last minute. It is by no means inconceivable that a premature accident or malfunction could put one boat out of commission, either permanently or for a long interval before this time. Furthermore, it is not simply a matter of the hulls remaining seaworthy. As they get older they will take longer to repair and re-fit, and maintenance will become more expensive. They will also get noisier and, in order to avoid undue wear and tear, will be confined to smaller patrol areas so becoming more vulnerable to Soviet anti-submarine warfare, which will probably have improved significantly by the 1990s. Once one boat becomes unserviceable it will be virtually impossible to keep another on station at all times. As a deterrent the force will lose much credibility.

It was difficult to be precise on how age would affect the different component parts of the nuclear force – missile motors, the wiring and reactor pressure vessel of the submarine. The best target date was provided by the fifth of the long re-fits for the first two submarines, scheduled for the early 1990s. Assuming that they would be due for replacement somewhere around that time it would seem prudent, if any replacement was deemed necessary, to avoid the expense of a re-fit.

In order to have a replacement ready by the early 1990s, a decision on the matter would have to be taken by the early 1980s. it is normally assumed that the time from conception to operation of a major new weapons system is at least a decade and perhaps longer. In what is now recognised to have been a very efficiently run programme, benefiting from transfers of American technology and equipment, it took just under 8 years for the December 1962 decision to purchase *Polaris* and for the fourth of the *Polaris* submarines to go on patrol. It would be difficult to construct four nuclear submarines, incorporating the technical advances made since the 1960s, as quickly as before. In the 1960s there were two shipyards – Barrow and Birkenhead – equipped to build nuclear-powered submarines. Now only Barrow is available, and that will be busy building hunter–killer submarines.

NON-DECISIONS

The replacement issue was brought to the public's attention by the publication in October 1977 of an independent report by the Royal Institute of International Affairs on the future of the British nuclear force, written by Ian Smart, the Institute's Deputy Director, on the basis of work undertaken in a study group which included the present author but excluded, at official insistence, informed civil servants. This report, more than any Government statements, set the terms of the debate for the late 1970s. Smart's conclusion was:

> If the British choice is to be the best and freest possible, it must be made . . . in at least some sense, by about 1980. Any delay beyond that time will entail increasing constraints, increasing costs and increasing risks.[6]

The necessity for urgent deliberation on the future of *Polaris* was not accepted by the Government, which argued that the matter raised by Ian Smart and others was, for the moment, a non-issue. In March 1978 the Secretary of State for Defence, Fred Mulley, explained that: 'In our view the existing *Polaris* fleet will be effective for many years and, that being the case, there is no need to take a decision on whether any other arrangements would have to be made.'[7] In a debate in the House of Lords, in May 1978, Lord Winterbottom made a similar point: 'The *Polaris* fleet has many years of effective life ahead of·it. There is no need for a decision to be taken about what may happen thereafter.'[8]

In early 1979, a Parliamentary Committee began to investigate the *Polaris* replacement problem. Unfortunately its inquiry had to be aborted because of the May General Election, before it had time to develop a considered view, but not before it had collected a substantial amount of evidence. The Ministry of Defence, in one of the slighter contributions to the proceedings, offered its 'present assessment' that 'the force can remain in service into the 1990s', observing how it would be misleading to give a 'single precise date when the *Polaris* force will cease to be operational, since the decision when to pay off the submarines must depend upon continuing careful assessment of their condition and that of their missiles and other equipment'. Mr Mulley, being examined by the Committee, did not (and could not) dissent from the Prime Minister who had said at question time on that day that a decision on replacement 'would need to be taken in the next two years', although he re-stated later on in his basic position that 'between 1979 and the early 1990s there is quite a chunk of time'.[9]

By this time the main concern was that the decision did not have to be taken prior to the General Election. Indeed, for public consumption, the Government might have wished that the decision could be postponed until 1985. Then it would not even be a matter for the next Government and so could be left out of the manifesto altogether. This was not possible. The Labour Party Manifesto included a passage on the issue, in which the option of authorising a successor was only just kept open, suggesting that a future public debate might just reverse the Party's established position:

In 1974, we renounced any intention of moving towards the production of a new generation of nuclear weapons or a successor to the *Polaris* nuclear force; we reiterate our belief that this is the best course for Britain. But many great issues affecting our allies and the world are involved, and a new round of Strategic Arms Limitation negotiations will soon begin. We think it is essential that there must be a full and informed debate about these issues in the country before any decision is taken.[10]

While there was an effort to postpone a public debate until after the election, a more exclusive discussion did take place within Government. Around the middle of 1977 the Ministry of Defence suggested that the problem required consideration. This was about the time of the publication of the report of the Royal Institute of International Affairs on the matter, but this may have been coincidence. As normal in these matters, the Prime Minister convened a small, private *ad hoc* group to consider these studies. This was outside the formal Cabinet structure (it even lacked a *Gen* number, used for subcommittees in Labour Cabinets). The Committee was composed of Prime Minister Callaghan; Denis Healey, Chancellor of the Exchequer; David Owen, Foreign Secretary; and Fred Mulley, Defence Secretary.

The committee requested studies on this matter from two working parties established in Whitehall which began work in January 1978: Sir Anthony Duff, Deputy Under-Secretary at the Foreign Office, chaired one on the military and international implications of a successor for *Polaris*; Professor Ronald Mason, Chief Scientific Adviser to the Ministry of Defence, chaired another on alternative delivery systems.[11] The Ministry of Defence was pleased to have control over the 'nuts and bolts' aspects of the review. Ministers made clear that the studies were to be undertaken without commitment and that recommendations were not required, only the considered views of senior officials on the available options. The few officials taking part – from the FCO, MOD, Treasury and the Cabinet Assessment Staff – were not to be seen as representing the views of their ministers. Nor did the ministers wish to see the papers produced by the groups until the studies had been completed. The work of these groups was, however, monitored by a group of Whitehall 'mandarins', chaired by Sir John Hunt, Secretary to the Cabinet, and including the Permanent Under-Secretaries of the Foreign Office, Treasury and Ministry of Defence (Sir Michael Palliser, Sir Douglas Wass and Sir Frank Cooper), the Chief of Defence Staff, Air Marshal Sir Neil Cameron, and Sir Clive Rose of the Cabinet Secretariat.

The working parties met regularly, putting together available information on all the options. The groups discussed the broad strategic, political, arms control, and, to some limited extent, budgetary implications of a replacement decision. A future force, it was noted, might not follow the 'Moscow criterion' (followed in the *Chevaline* programme) but make do with an ability to attack some nine major cities other than the capital. As for hardware, air-launched and ground-launched systems were virtually ruled out, but the various sea-launched options were kept open.

During the course of these studies, the Cabinet subcommittee of four met rarely, and then only to consider arms control and NATO nuclear matters. It did not address the replacement issue properly until two inconclusive meetings of November 1978, as each of the two working parties reported. No firm consensus came out of this but some clear themes were starting to emerge. The first of these was that the optimum date for a decision was around the end of 1980, and the second, that if a replacement was considered necessary it should probably be a submarine-based system.

There was concern over the costs of a new force. Foreign Secretary, David Owen, for example, while wishing to retain a nuclear capability, was worried that the Ministry of Defence was so anxious to get the best possible successor force that it was ignoring perfectly satisfactory and cheaper, if less impressive, alternatives such as cruise missiles on attack submarines or keeping the existing force in service for longer. Mr Mulley, reflecting the views of his Ministry, argued back that the cruise missile option was possibly more expensive than his preferred successor of ballistic-missile-carrying submarines.

No ministerial decisions on the matter were taken. The possibility that a replacement would be necessary and that if so, it would probably require American help, was sufficient to allow Mr Callaghan, whose instincts were in favour of replacement, to raise the issue tentatively with President Carter during the Guadeloupe summit of early January 1979. Little was done on the matter after that because of the country's industrial disorder and the build-up to the May General Election. However, a hint of Ministry of Defence thinking was made available to the Defence and External Affairs Subcommittee of the Expenditure Committee looking into nuclear weapons policy.

Although a sizeable amount of detailed staff work had been undertaken, the Ministry's evidence to the Expenditure Committee belies the existence of a corpus of knowledge on the question of succession. Because there were no plans for a successor, it was suggested, all questions on the most appropriate type of system and its cost, were 'hypothetical' or 'theoretical'. All that was provided was a list of factors that would have to be taken into account, were this matter to somehow become a live issue. But even a list of questions can reflect a train of thought. Reading between the lines of the Ministry's evidence a consensus can be detected pointing to a submarine-based system as the most appropriate successor, if possible drawing, as with *Polaris*, on American know-how and hardware. A shared system 'would avoid very considerable expenditure in research and development and help to reduce unit costs and to produce savings in subsequent in-service logistic support'.[12]

The fact that the Government had not ruled out a replacement for *Polaris* was made clear by Defence Secretary Fred Mulley, himself equivocal on the issue although convinced that any successor would have to be a ballistic missile rather than a cruise missile system.

In a debate on defence in the Commons just before the 1979 Election campaign he remarked:

> I could not say today that in no circumstances would I be in favour of moving towards a new generation. I accept that the arguments for and against are very finely balanced. The answer depends a great deal on what happens in the next year or two.[13]

DECISIONS

The Conservative victory in May 1979 brought to office a Government committed to the nuclear deterrent. Even before a decision had been taken on the manner of the replacement of *Polaris*, ministers made it clear publicly that there would be some replacement. In all analyses of the problem within the Government it was virtually taken as given that there would be some successor.

One of the first of the Cabinet subcommittees set up by the Government was MISC 7 (Conservative special committees are designated MISC – for 'Miscellaneous'). MISC 7 consisted of Prime Minister Margaret Thatcher and Home Secretary William Whitelaw, the Chancellor Geoffrey Howe and the Defence and Foreign Secretaries, Francis Pym and Lord Carrington. The committee of senior officials was also re-formed. This group was concerned with issues other than *Polaris* replacement. For example, one of its first tasks was to confirm the British negotiating position on NATO's Theatre Nuclear Force Modernisation. However, the British nuclear force was the priority.

In this, the group was able to move quickly, benefiting from the work undertaken during the previous administration. It received the papers from the Duff and Mason working groups, amended to take account of the fact that a new Government was in opposition. In October, the Defence Secretary promised that:

> We will go on improving the *Polaris* force so that it will remain an ultimate deterrent to aggression in the 1990s. Furthermore consideration is already being given to the action that will be necessary to continue our strategic deterrent capability for as long as necessary thereafter.[14]

By October 1979 the views of most of the interested parties in Whitehall had been canvassed. The Chiefs of Staff, under the chairmanship of Admiral Sir Terence Lewin, endorsed a successor force although some of the chiefs were nervous about the budgetary consequences for the conventional forces. (This is not an issue on which the military traditionally take the lead, although serious dissent from a particular proposal can be influential.) MISC 7 was moving to the position that the *Polaris* force should be replaced in the early 1990s by a new submarine-launched missile system.[15] However, no firm decisions were taken.

The Government expected more public debate on the matter than in fact materialised, and it conducted its decision-making as to the preferred successor on this basis. One participant described it as a 'painstaking attempt not to be seen to be jumping to the obvious conclusion'. Despite the clear movement in policy all the options were kept formally open, and the Treasury asked the proper questions on the financial and budgetary implications.

In terms of hardware, the cruise missile was falling out of favour, but those anxious about the cost of a new system were urging consideration of less expensive options than the Ministry of Defence's candidate – the American *Trident 1* SLBM. The alternative was an upgraded *Polaris*, adding to the old missiles elements taken from the more modern *Poseidon* and *Trident*. After the costly experience of *Chevaline*, in which the development costs had shot up, to mock the early estimates, the Ministry of Defence remained dubious about whether an upgraded *Polaris* would be cheaper than *Trident*.

THE FRENCH CONNECTION

One option that was not thoroughly considered was that of collaboration with France. This was largely for practical reasons. Although the French are developing a new MIRVed missile – the M-4 – which might be an attractive option with which to replace *Polaris*, so much in Britain's nuclear programme is related to the American programme that any attempts to graft on a French missile would face problems of compatibility in related systems, as well as possibly contravening the regulations governing the supply of information from the United States to Britain. In addition, American missiles would be much less expensive. Apart from missiles, Britain's indigenous nuclear submarine and warhead technology is ahead of that of France. Moreover, the British and French forces have been operating on a completely different basis, with the *Polaris* fleet assigned to NATO and the 'force de frappe' kept strictly separate from the alliance.

However, there has been evidence of serious concern within France over the difficulty of maintaining an independent nuclear deterrent for the rest of this century. Without the American assistance enjoyed by Britain, France has had to devote considerable effort and resources to the development of its nuclear forces, in a programme that has been beset by technical difficulties and delays. While Britain has been spending only a small percentage of its defence budget on nuclear forces, France has been spending 15–20 per cent. For this extra expense France has achieved a triad of forces – the *Mirage IV* aircraft as well as land-based and sea-based missiles. But the *Mirage* is almost as old as Britain's *Vulcan* bombers and is handicapped by its limited range and inability to penetrate Soviet air defences. The 18 land-based ballistic missiles are vulnerable to a surprise attack from the Soviet Union, particularly now that its own MIRVed and accurate SS-20 is in place. The French Ministry of Defence has been engaged in a major review to see whether anything can be done for the land-based force, but it is generally accepted that future effort will have to be concentrated on the sea-based missiles. The construction of this component of the French force has been somewhat prolonged. *Le Redoutable*, the first boat, was laid down in 1964, the same year as *Resolution*, the first of the British boats, but it did not become operational until 1971, three years after

Resolution. A four-boat force was not available until 1977, 7 years after Britain. The French are intending to have more submarines than Britain: the fifth boat, *Le Tonnant,* is due to come in service in 1980 and a sixth, *L'inflexible,* in 1985. It is not clear whether this new boat is to be the end of the old series or the start of a new series.

The French have often been forced to scale down their nuclear plans and may have to do so in the future. They have spoken boldly about MIRVs, cruise missiles, surveillance satellites and neutron bombs, but budgetary realities intervene. This has put the Government in an awkward position for the 'force de frappe' figures prominently in contemporary French mythology along with associated symbolic measures such as the withdrawal from NATO's integrated military command. French politicians have been proud to brag about the nuclear achievement, claiming to be the 'third nuclear power' (which the British dispute). Unfortunately, it is an expensive and technically demanding business and there have been recent signs of an interest in sharing some of the burden with European partners. In August 1979 two Gaullists, General George Buis and Alexandre Sanguinetti, published an article suggesting a Franco-German nuclear force (thus horrifying that section of the French political and military establishment which believes Germany to be as much a likely target as the Soviet Union). In January 1980, M Michel Poniatowski, a close associate of President Giscard d'Estaing and a former Minister of the Interior, floated the idea of a joint French and British force acting for Europe. These ideas reflect French unease over the long-term viability of its own force but are always politically somewhat unrealistic, for instance in requiring the would-be partner to leave NATO.

Nor have these ideas ever received official endorsement. Nevertheless, both the recent Labour and Conservative Governments in Britain have received extremely discreet feelers from the French on possible areas of cooperation. French Defence Minister Yvon Bourges was reported to have suggested to his opposite number in Britain, Fred Mulley, that there might be possibilities for collaboration in the development and construction of hulls for nuclear submarines. As Britain's official policy was not yet one of *Polaris* replacement Mr Mulley made it clear there was little immediate point in pursuing the idea.

When the Conservatives won the election in May 1979 the

French again made discreet approaches, hoping that the new, more enthusiastic attitudes towards the European Community, as well as towards nuclear forces, would result in a positive response. Before the election French officials had discussed the matter with Conservative MPs and had gained the impression that the intention was to explore cooperation with the United States but, if that failed, to consider cooperation with France. In post-election conversations, the British noted a clear French interest in cooperation, though few details were discussed. The impression was gained that if Britain were interested the French would prefer it to make the first official move because of their domestic political problems with the issue, and the need for the British to square any deal with the Americans. By equally discreet means, the British explained that they saw little benefit for themselves in collaboration, and that the economic and political costs would be high.

THE SPECIAL RELATIONSHIP

However European in foreign policy, the Conservatives felt that the past relationship with the United States made it the obvious source of future help. What is remarkable about the positive nature of the American response was the extent to which it contrasted with the approach of the Kennedy Administration of 18 years before. The bitterness generated within the alliance as a result of the American opposition to independent nuclear forces had done so much damage, without resolving the issues at stake, that later Administrations had come to accept that little could be gained by dwelling on the matter. Moreover, familiarity breeds indifference and as the British and French nuclear forces became established they began to blend into the strategic landscape. Meanwhile, American views on doctrine became less self-confident and arrogant.

Once removed from the doctrinal controversy the positive virtues of the special nuclear relationship with Britain came to the fore. When, prior to the May 1979 election, American officials began to consider appropriate responses to a British request for assistance, it was soon concluded that a request should be treated positively, not as an act of charity but because of wider political and strategic benefits.

The United States still found its own *Polaris* base at Holy Loch valuable, and felt it might be put in jeopardy if British requests for assistance were frustrated. It remained useful to have another informed and friendly power to talk with on technical and nuclear matters. The British force boosted NATO's nuclear position in the European theatre and must cause some uncertainty in the Soviet mind, so adding to deterrence. To the extent that possession of nuclear weapons helped maintain Britain's faltering international position, this was an additional argument for being responsive, for Britain was still regarded as a particularly sympathetic ally. The American Defense Department report of January 1980 contains, for the first time, a positive endorsement of the British force: 'The close US cooperation with this capability reflects our judgement that the British force, which is committed to NATO, contributes to our mutual defense interests.'[16] By contrast, the French force, which is not committed to NATO, merely gets a mention.

Despite this, the political climate in Washington is notably variable. Even as Mrs Thatcher was persuading President Carter to aid Britain in extending the power of its nuclear arsenal, she did not enjoy similar success on the question of making available American rifles for the Royal Ulster Constabulary. SALT might have provided problems, were it not for the fact that President Carter almost welcomed an opportunity to demonstrate to his critics that the 1979 SALT agreement did not impede cooperation with allies. At other times resurgent concern over nuclear proliferation or irritation with Europe in general, might have caused problems. The virtual absence of any serious opposition in Washington to strategic assistance to Britain made this an extremely good moment for the Prime Minister to press the issue.

In December 1979, Mrs Thatcher was able to ask the Americans for assistance when she visited President Carter (although initial soundings had been taken by Francis Pym when he visited his opposite number in Washington, Harold Brown, in July). The communiqué after the Thatcher–Carter summit noted agreement 'on the importance of maintaining a credible British strategic deterrent and US/UK strategic cooperation', and that the two countries 'should continue their discussions of the most appropriate means of achieving these objectives for the future.'[17] The 'continuing' discussions referred to in the communiqué were not detailed negotiations on the purchase of *Trident* but rather a series of American responses to British requests for information on the characteristics of a variety of weapons systems. Even having agreed cooperation in principle, the British were kept waiting by Washington for the agreement to announce the specific form the cooperation would take. President Carter wished to secure his own political position, at least to the point of beating off the challenge of Senator Kennedy. In addition, the uncertainty in détente and SALT following the Soviet invasion of Afghanistan affected all areas of policy. There was some concern that a public announcement of US–UK strategic cooperation might be assigned far more immediate international significance than it in fact deserved. There may have been some uncertainty about the appropriate price. Thus, London had to wait until Washington suggested that the time was ripe for a formal British request.

On 24 January 1980, in the first parliamentary debate on the nuclear force for 15 years, Mr Pym made clear the Government's determination to find a successor to *Polaris*. Although he did not name the successor, insisting that this still had to be decided, his estimate of the costs of the new programme (£4–5 billion) and, more pertinently, the comments by Mr Barney Hayhoe, the Under-Secretary of Defence for the Army, replying for the Government at the end of the debate, made it clear that cruise missiles had not impressed and that a submarine-based ballistic missile was the preferred option.[18] One feature of the debate was the muted response of the Labour Party opposition to the announcement. The Shadow Defence Secretary William Rodgers declared himself to be 'agnostic' and unconvinced 'by the robust certainty of others'. The major issue he and his colleagues raised was of the budgetary impact of a new nuclear force. There was a greater source of unease over expense than the effects on the arms race and the morality of it all.

At the time of writing (February 1980) the choice of *Trident 1* has yet to be officially confirmed as the successor to *Polaris*. It would, however, be very surprising if an announcement to this effect did not come at some point in 1980. Inevitably, in the absence of an announcement there has been speculation that the Government is baulking at the cost of *Trident* and is searching for a cheaper alternative. To appreciate the probable choice to be made by the Government and its full implications it is now necessary to put the decision in its strategic, political and economic context.

7 Cruise Missiles *versus* Ballistic Missiles

The main surprise, and disappointment, for many people in the choice of a successor to *Polaris* was that it is to be another ballistic missile rather than a cruise missile. The cruise missile is a pilotless aircraft with continuous propulsion, the descendant of the V-1 'buzz' bomb. Of Hitler's two 'revenge' weapons, the comparatively unsophisticated V-1 was less expensive and therefore more efficient than the complicated V-2 ballistic missile. The V-2 could penetrate defences much more easily, but each missile was enormously expensive. Nevertheless, it was the progeny of the V-2 that came to occupy the central place in the arsenals of the super-powers after the war.

Both in the United States and the Soviet Union cruise missiles were developed in the 1950s, but they were cumbersome to operate, vulnerable to defences and highly inaccurate. In the 1960s, they came to be superseded by ballistic missiles in all but short-range tactical roles. Because the Soviet Union took longer to develop a submarine-launched ballistic missile force, it operated a much more substantial submarine-based cruise missile force. It still has around 100 of these missiles (designated SS-N-3) but they have a range of no more than 600 kilometres, and require surface launch, rendering their carriers vulnerable to attack.

The United States became interested in cruise missiles again in the early 1970s for two reasons. First, new technologies offered the possibility of overcoming the past disadvantages of those missiles which stemmed from high fuel consumption, innacuracy and small payload. Advances in the design of munitions and jet engines, and in high-energy fuel chemistry, now allow for a cruise missile to pack an effective punch at long ranges. Furthermore, modern guidance technology now permits extremely high accuracies. A combination of inertial navigation and Terrain Contour Matching (TERCOM), which enables the missile to recognise and adjust to the terrain on the approach to its targets, promises accuracies of a few metres.

The second factor which encouraged interest in cruise missiles was the fact that it was not mentioned in the SALT I agreement of May 1972, limiting offensive arms. This mentioned only ballistic missiles. In the Pentagon it was noted that the old Soviet SS-N-3s, which could still just about reach American cities if they ventured far enough into the Atlantic Ocean, were unrestrained by SALT and unmatched by the United States. An opportunity was seen to expand American forces in an interesting new area without violating SALT I. Dr Henry Kissinger, advising President Nixon, supported the new programme as a possible bargaining counter with the Soviet Union in the next round of SALT negotiations.

However, a new weapon which incorporated all the advances in military technology was not going to be easily bargained away. Soon it was getting a reputation as being quite revolutionary, accurate, inexpensive and versatile. It was able to perform in strategic or tactical roles, to be fitted with conventional or nuclear warheads, to operate at short or long ranges, and to be independent of any particular launch platform. The more the Russians attempted to impede its development at SALT, the more its reputation grew. President Carter in June 1977 decided that by fitting air-launched cruise missiles to the ageing B-52 bombers he could be spared the expense of producing a new bomber – the B-1. The cruise missile was now established as the low-cost alternative to the traditional nuclear delivery vehicles.

THE VITAL OPTION

By the mid-1970s, European interest had been roused, and the cruise missile was being canvassed as preferable to a ballistic missile for a small nuclear force. An example of this enthusiasm can be found in a book published in Britain in 1977 by James Bellini and Geoffrey Pattie MP (now Under-Secretary for the RAF). This contained a chapter entitled: 'Cruise Missile: Britain's Vital Option'.[1]

In Britain, studies of the technical qualities of cruise missiles began in 1974–5, with the close links with the American research establishment being put to use unofficially in order to find out how serious a breakthrough had been made. As in the United States the military by no means embraced the cruise missile concept. Some, in the RAF for example, worried lest it one day replace piloted aircraft on conventional missions. Studies also began at British Aerospace Dynamics at Stevenage. In 1976 these were picked up by the Ministry of Defence and contracts were issued worth £130,000 (£10,500 in 1977/8 and £120,000 in 1978/9 budgets). This was in addition to work already being undertaken on a short-range cruise missile with a conventional warhead for an anti-shipping role. The new study involved no more than a couple of dozen people, and was completed in late 1978. It was quite preliminary to any serious research and development. It did, however, involve examination of all the features of a modern cruise missile, including TERCOM guidance. The purpose of the study was described in July 1977 as being to clarify 'some of the options and limitations which would be involved in the possible development of a weapons system'. Mr Mulley was not very pleased about these studies, when he discovered their existence, because of the political problems they might create. He described the studies in public as being 'limited', intended 'to enable us to participate in NATO discussions on the defence potential and arms control implications of these systems'.[2]

Mr Mulley's description played down the extent to which the value of cruise missiles as a strategic nuclear system for Britain was under investigation. The result of the British Aerospace study was to suggest that if the cruise missile route was to be followed this was within indigenous capabilities and that the best course might be to skip the current stage of American development of sub-sonic cruise missiles and move straight on to a super-sonic version. However, in these studies and those carried out in the 1978 working group on options for *Polaris* replacement under the chairmanship of Sir Ronald Mason, basic problems with cruise missiles came to be emphasised.

The appearance of low cost had been created by comparing the price of a single cruise missile (under £1 million) with that of a single ballistic missile (up to £6 million), and then by assuming that the cost to Britain would be the same as that to the United States, which could draw on a vast technological base.

On this latter point one good example was the TERCOM

guidance system. This requires up-to-date topographical information, which in turn requires reconnaissance satellites. (When
France was undergoing a burst of enthusiasm on cruise missiles it
accepted that it would have to develop its own satellites.) A
Congressional committee in America was told in 1977 that the
cost of acquiring topographic data and the digitising of maps for
TERCOM, which works by comparing the terrain it is passing
over with a map in its nose-cone, was 'extraordinarily greater'
than the cost of the missile itself.[3] It would, of course, be possible to
do without the high accuracy of TERCOM, but that would
involve doing without one of the major features of this new system.

The long-range cruise missile currently being tested in the
United States has two major drawbacks. First, it carries only a
single warhead, so a smaller number of targets can be attacked by
an individual weapon than by a multiple-warhead ballistic missile. Second, it travels slowly at sub-sonic speed. This means that
it is potentially vulnerable to air defence. While existing Soviet air
defences could not cope particularly well with cruise missiles
because of the low altitudes at which they fly, the problems are not
insuperable. As the United States will be deploying a lot of cruise
missiles of its own it is expected that the Soviet Union will respond
by improving its air defences to cope with this new threat. It is
anticipated in the United States that high-value targets will only
be reached by saturating rather than penetrating defences. This
will require many extra missiles. American scientists have already
been contemplating a second-generation cruise missile with a
much smaller radar signature, but this indicates the extent to
which reliance on cruise missiles by Britain would involve dependence on an unsettled technology, in which it could easily become
committed to an obsolete system.

It is normally assumed that the ballistic missile's problems are
slight in comparison, because of the speed and variability of its
flight, and because of the immensely useful SALT I Treaty
limiting ABMs. This assumption remains reasonable. However,
it should be noted that the ABM Treaty could be abrogated,
either in the total unravelling of the SALT process, or in an
American move to protect its land-based deterrent without going
to the expense and bother of a new mobile ICBM. Abrogation or
amendment of the ABM Treaty for this latter purpose would not
by itself cause drastic problems because protection of missile
bases would not protect cities, the basic targets of a British force,

but it would certainly introduce a new element of uncertainty into British calculations. (Even within the Treaty limits, improvements to the Soviet ABM force could cause some difficulties.)

The question of the most appropriate launch platform for cruise missiles is similar to that for ballistic missiles. Although cruise missiles are smaller, both types can in principle be based on the ground, on aircraft, or on submarines. In an age of increasingly accurate missiles a small force cannot afford to be in a fixed base. They can then become vulnerable to surprise attack and so lose a major qualification as a retaliatory system. This almost rules out aircraft as well as missiles placed in protected silos. Aircraft can survive surprise attack, but this requires a significant number being kept on airborne alert, which is extremely expensive. Surface ships are vulnerable to modern anti-ship weapons.

The Americans are preparing their cruise missiles to be mobile and ground-launched for deployment *en masse* in Europe from 1983 on. Britain is to be host to 160 of these ground-launched cruise missiles (GLCMs) on bases already used by the US Air Force. It has been suggested that rather than move to a new generation of ballistic missiles, Britain should purchase a number of GLCMs. As we shall see (in Chapter 11), the possibility of a British GLCM force was seriously considered, but as a complement to *Polaris* and not as a replacement – a contribution to NATO's long-range theatre nuclear forces and not as a strategic deterrent.

GLCMs that had to be launched from Britain would not be suitable for this second role. Not only would they lack the range to attack much beyond the western districts of the Soviet Union, but they would be vulnerable to a surprise attack. The proposed NATO system is mobile, but except at a time of dire emergency the missiles are to be on base and not wandering around the country. The security problems if they were allowed to so wander would be enormous. Even then, the Soviet Union would be able to bombard the area in which the missile would probably be found. In the case of the role for which NATO is introducing these missiles, this weakness is mitigated by the fact that they would be put on alert early in a war, and, if nuclear weapons are to be employed, they will be used before the central strategic systems. Moreover, the nuclear bombardment of a large part of Europe would cause so much death and destruction that it could warrant a full-scale nuclear retaliation by NATO. The value of long-range theatre forces thus depends on the existence of a 'last-resort', survivable force. It is not an alternative to such a force.

The NATO planners had considered putting cruise missiles into submarines, but this was ruled out both on political and military grounds. It was felt to be important to have weapons on the ground in Europe, in the path of any invasion and thus committed to its obstruction, rather than in the sea able to creep away from the fighting. Submarine-basing would also be much more expensive. On the other hand it was accepted that if the main objective was survivability this would be an appropriate basing mode. For a strategic deterrent survivability is a prime objective. But once cruise missiles are carried underwater, their costs rise beyond those of ballistic missiles.

Eventually submarines may become vulnerable to anti-submarine warfare (ASW) but this still appears to be distant. The history of ASW has been one of gradual, slow, incremental improvement in which the West has remained far ahead of the East. The sea is still a relatively unknown environment and man has yet to make it transparent. The principal sensing medium in ASW remains sound. Sound not only travels more slowly than light, but is created by the hunter as well as the hunted. This makes it possible for a boat enjoying a sonar advantage to be warned of an approaching attacker. Even then it is one thing to detect and follow an enemy submarine; it is quite another thing to do this when the moment comes to execute a pre-emptive strike. So, the incentives for staying underwater are strong.

More missiles mean more submarines, and it is submarines not missiles which constitute the most expensive component of the system. In his 1977 report, which did much to dispel illusions in this area, Ian Smart estimated the cruise missile force equivalent in destructive effect to five submarines, each carrying 16 modern ballistic missiles with three warheads of 170 kilotons each. Assuming that no more than half the single-warhead cruise missiles would reach their targets, the number needed to attack the same number of targets as two ballistic-missile submarines on station would be 192. Then assuming that no more than 24 cruise missiles can be carried on each submarine, eight submarines would have to be on station at any time. As these submarines would also have to be maintained and re-fitted, 17 would be required.[4] To produce so many boats on schedule would require an expansion of shipyard capacity. To operate them would require expansion of base facilities and many more men, when sailors prepared to spend 2 months at a stretch undersea are becoming a scarce commodity. Estimates on this by the Ministry of Defence suggested that even more boats might be needed. The smaller size of cruise missiles would allow for less expensive individual submarines, but even so the total force would probably cost a lot more than a ballistic missile force.

One impressive piece of testimony was provided by British Aerospace Dynamics in their evidence to the Expenditure Committee. After expressing 'confidence that we can develop a cruise missile system acting as prime contractor in a national programme', when it came to choosing the most 'effective' system it noted: 'On the information available to us at present, we would expect that a ballistic missile would be more likely to be the one appropriate to the needs of the UK.'[5]

The case against this was based on the fact that the Americans' original intention had been to fit cruise missiles into the torpedo tubes of attack submarines. Britain already has a number of nuclear-powered attack submarines, and so would be able to save in the development of new types. Moreover, if all that was desired was some serious and assured retaliatory capability then it was not necessary to insist on as much destructive potential as that carried on the current *Polaris* force. Something substantially less would suffice as long as it was available for a second strike, requiring only, say, three submarines to be on station at any time. This argument had little currency in the Ministry of Defence, but it did find some support in the Foreign Office, particularly while Dr David Owen was Foreign Secretary. It is of note that after he had been minister responsible for the Navy in 1968-70, Dr Owen suggested that a British force need only be sufficient to make a contribution to NATO and not necessarily to act independently. He argued that the 1964 decision to have four boats, so at least one was on station at all times 'lost a unique opportunity to kill once and for all the whole concept of a separate British national deterrent'.[6]

The problems with dual-capable attack submarines, as with dual-capable aircraft, is that they are often wanted for both the alternative roles at the same time. When the submarines were most wanted for anti-submarine activities they would be required to be on station and acting as a deterrent. Admirals would be scared to commit them to a conventional engagement lest a substantial chunk of the nuclear force was lost in the action. Separateness and survivability are virtues in a nuclear force. If it were caught in a conventional attack this could be misinterpreted as a determined assault on the deterrent.

A minimal cruise missile force would provide a slight return for what would still be a substantial expenditure in a venture with serious risks of going wrong. In addition, the Americans were losing interest in submarine-launched cruise missiles of their own so Britain would be able to draw less on their experience and technology. Furthermore, as there are less than ten torpedo tubes on each attack submarine, a new type of submarine would have to be designed to take the optimal number of cruise missiles. The preference was to follow the known and safer path of ballistic missiles.

TRIDENT

Having chosen ballistic missiles, it was not inevitable that *Trident* would be the preferred system. As the need for a new force was caused by the decline of the submarines rather than the missiles, in principle the existing *Polaris* A-3 missile, or some modified version, could have been kept going, buying up the American stocks when they took *Polaris* out of service. For British needs *Polaris* should remain quite adequate for some time, and the country has recently spent considerable sums devising and producing a new warhead. As the cruise missile option declined, those anxious for a cheaper missile than *Trident* demanded careful consideration of an 'up-rated *Polaris*'.

The difficulty here lies in holding on alone to a 1960s technology well into the next century. Maintenance, spare parts and, most of all, compatibility with the technological environment in which one is operating would make life increasingly difficult and expensive. It would be like owning a serviceable vintage car, but without the charm. To try to incorporate modern parts into the missile might result only in a difficult and expensive development effort. Furthermore, as the main cost of the new system will lie with the submarines rather than the missiles the savings would not necessarily be particularly large.

In buying a new missile, the advantage lies with the type that is both modern and proven. This points to the new *Trident* C-4 SLBM. This missile is now entering service with the US Navy after a successful testing programme. It is first taking over from

Poseidon on ten existing submarines, before appearing on a new boat capable of carrying 24 missiles.

Trident has been designed with American rather than British needs in mind. This is most evident in its range of 4000 nautical miles (4600 statute miles). *Polaris*'s 2500 nautical miles gives Britain adequate target coverage. The value of *Trident*'s extra range is in allowing greater flexibility in employment. A vast array of targets could be attacked without moving from the Faslane base, while on moving out to sea a much larger patrol area becomes available. This increased ability to move around in a large expanse of water, so complicating the enemy's submarine hunting efforts, is an important benefit of a longer-range missile.

The most significant change in moving from *Polaris* to *Trident* lies in the warhead. The British will produce their own warhead. It may well be tempted to follow the American design, as much as permissible, which would result in a MIRVed front-end, with eight warheads of 100 kilotons each. This would represent a major leap in sophistication, meaning that, with 16 missiles per boat, each of the new submarines would be able to hit twice as many separated targets as the whole of the existing *Polaris* fleet. Something less complicated and capable would do, and it has been authoritatively stated that Britain has an indigenous capability for developing MIRVs of its own design. But here again the cost of not following the American line of development may result in lower quality for greater price. The *Chevaline* programme demonstrated the cost-disadvantage of experimenting alone, even when something technically competent is eventually produced. Unfortunately, the new warhead developed for *Polaris* will probably not be suitable for *Trident*, which can carry a load three times as great.

Where the American line of development will not be followed is in submarine design. The new, 24-missile *Trident* submarines are being criticised for their unduly large size. This allows them to travel long distances, but with 4000 mile range missiles it is possible to stay close to coastal waters, less contested by the enemy. They have been surrounded by construction problems in the US shipyards, resulting in delays and cost overruns.

It has been suggested that Britain would be wise to move in the opposite direction with smaller submarines operating close to coastal waters, perhaps with conventional rather than nuclear power plants. The waters around Britain are not congenial for Soviet anti-submarine activities, while the range of the *Trident* is such that there is no need to stray far from home. This idea has not received a warm response from the Ministry of Defence. This may be because of the reluctance of naval architects to resist an opportunity to produce the most advanced submarine possible. More legitimately, it may reflect the phenomenon we have already noticed: the reluctance to experiment in a programme with only slight margins for error. Attempting to accommodate a number of missiles as large as the *Trident* in a small vessel may pose serious engineering problems. One problem would be in having enough power for the complicated electrics connected with missile firing. While diesel engines can be generally less noisy the need of submarines so powered to take in air requires pushing up the snort above the surface, at which point detection becomes possible. This operation is in itself noisy. Furthermore, lots of boats would complicate command and control problems, with multiple centres of button-pressing, while the need to rely on more junior officers and ratings and to operate close to coastal waters could increase the risk of accidents.

It is most likely that the submarine will follow those constructed for *Polaris* with nuclear power and carrying 16 missiles. This time, five boats will probably be built rather than four to ensure that at least two boats can be on station all the time, although the Treasury has been questioning the necessity of this. If the most modern type of power plants are used, it may be possible to operate the boats for longer periods without major re-fits, in which case up to three boats could be on station at times (although this has not been the determining factor in the past). If so desired a new power plant might last for up to 10 years without re-fuelling. The development of a new unit for a ballistic missile submarine will probably be influenced by development work already well under way on the propulsion for the next generation of nuclear-powered hunter-killer submarines. These have different needs – speed rather than a capacity for prolonged periods at sea – and carry less weight, but a similar plant could probably do for both.

The incentive to follow the previous system in all aspects is strong. It reduces problems of basing, training and general infrastructural costs. It is safer, if less exciting and bold, to follow familiar technologies and concepts rather than experiment with a bright idea that could go terribly wrong. If this programme fails it is unlikely that there will be the political will or available money for another try.

8   Defence Priorities

A decision to modernise the nuclear portion of Britain's armed forces is not in principle different from a decision to modernise other portions. It is quite usual for one capability to demand little more than the cost of operation and maintenance of existing equipment for many years before requiring a marked increase in allocations for new equipment. Every line item in a budget can expect to have peaks and troughs over the years. It is the art of managing a budget to ensure that too many peaks do not occur simultaneously. Thus, just because the nuclear force is going to cost more in the 1980s than in the 1970s, does not by itself mean that it can only be accommodated with a drastic effect elsewhere in the country's defence effort. The opportunity cost of nuclear forces in terms of conventional forces will depend on what else urgently needs to be done and the general level of resources available.

The nuclear force has kept its place in the defence budget over the years in part because it has not been abnormally burdensome. Since Nassau, there have been substantial and often sudden contractions in Britain's defence effort, cutting back on non-European activities to the minimal permitted by obligations to the residue of Empire. It is nevertheless hard to point to a decision to abandon a major conventional capability that was forced on a Government because of some desperate struggle to 'stay nuclear'. If the nuclear force itself had been abandoned in 1962, it is unlikely that the rest of the defence effort would look at all different now.

Compared with other items in the budget, the nuclear strategic force does not appear exorbitant, considering the relative punch it packs. The *Polaris* programme has been successful. The continuity of patrols has not been interrupted (Mr Pym reported 114 separate patrols in all by the start of 1980) despite some industrial troubles among the civilian personnel. The naval officers involved, and the crew, impress with their dedication and high morale, and they remain well trained. Some operational costs are less than those of the American *Polaris* boats. For example, while the American boats fire three test missiles after each long re-fit, the British fire only one.

Excluding R&D, the force currently costs about as much as the RAF spends on transport aircraft, less than the RN spends on submarines for non-nuclear missions, and less than an eighth of what the Army spends on BAOR. It is only when one looks at R&D that any sense of imbalance creeps in. Presuming that the heading 'other R&D' is largely composed of 'nuclear R&D', it absorbs more funds than all areas but military aircraft, taking up 16 per cent of the total R&D budget, while the item for nuclear strategic forces still represents only 1.5 per cent of the overall budget. Even a major new nuclear programme, however, will be of a comparable order to re-equipping the Army with tanks, or the RAF with front-line combat aircraft: expensive but, in defence terms, by no means outlandish.

Nevertheless, the sums involved are large enough to make any politician pause for thought. The moment of truth for any area of defence capability tends to come at the point of moving to the next generation of equipment, where the advance of military technology leads to cost estimates far in excess of the previous generation. The decisions in the 1960s not to acquire long-range strike aircraft or large aircraft carriers are examples of this, although in each case the abandonment has not been total. What was unusual about the nuclear force in the 1960s was that its modernisation had been accompanied by a marked reduction of costs. The same is unlikely to happen in the 1990s.

FUTURE COSTS

It is difficult to be precise about the future costs, and probably unwise to attempt to be so. Even official estimates at the start of new programmes rarely match the accounts produced at the end. Furthermore, the distribution of expenditure can matter as much as the absolute amounts involved.

In discussing *Polaris* replacement in the Commons in January

1980, Defence Secretary Francis Pym made a number of points concerning the cost. He offered, as a realistic estimate, 'a total capital cost in the range of £4000 million to £5000 million at today's prices'. To put this in perspective he then made a number of points: the spending would be spread over 10–15 years; the peak years of expenditure would probably come towards the end of the 1980s when it would absorb about 5 per cent of the defence budget; it would be of the same order of magnitude as (if anything less than) the current *Tornado* programme and much less than the construction of the V-bomber force in the 1950s.' Mr Pym did not disaggregate his figure for total capital costs. On past experience, the submarines will cost significantly more than the missiles and their associated equipment.

Research and development represents the 'high risk' element of the costs. The time and resources necessary to solve some of the trickier problems in advanced technology are hard to calculate; nor can there be any certainty of success. In the past delays in development have led not only to the rapid escalation of costs but also to the effective obsolescence of the system before it had been introduced. The result was cancellations and a massive waste of public money. Cancellations are part of the past history of the nuclear programme, with the *Blue Streak* (April 1960), *Skybolt* (December 1962), and the TSR-2 (April 1965). The advantage of a familiar technology is considerable in planning, even if initial cost estimates suggest it may be more expensive than a more experimental option. *Trident* as a missile is proven, and the problems of carrying missiles on modern nuclear submarines are well understood.

The second additional element in the cost estimates concerns the life-expectancy of the new systems and the regular operational and maintenance costs. A badly designed system, which has lots of 'teething troubles', or one that gets rapidly overtaken by improvements in Soviet counter-measures, or one that involves the extensive utilisation of equipment that is ageing, may soon be rendered ineffectual so that the problem of replacement comes to the fore again. This is another area where continuity brings benefits in that existing support facilities for basing, training, repairs and re-fits can be used.

Over time, the operation of a system comes to cost more than the original purchase of the hardware, so the annual operating costs are obviously an important factor in deciding on the overall cost-effectiveness of a new system. In 1973 the cost of an extra *Polaris* submarine was given as £90 million, with running costs at £8 million per annum, so it would have taken only 11 years for the cumulative operation and maintenance budget to have exceeded the original capital investment. Indeed, the costs for the *Polaris* force that was procured have now followed this pattern.

The *Polaris* fleet will have to be maintained while its replacement is being constructed. The replacement costs will thus be in addition to the maintenance costs of the existing force. These are expected to grow from 1.5 per cent to 2 per cent of the defence budget, which suggest a move, in 1980 prices, from around £130 million to an average of £185 million by the late 1980s. This is before any funds are expended on the new force.

One determinant of the distribution of costs will be shipyard capacity. Two yards – Barrow and Birkenhead – were available in the 1960s for *Polaris*. Only Barrow now has a capacity in this area and this is in demand for attack submarines. Unless this capacity is expanded, perhaps by rehabilitating the old Birkenhead yard (which was responsible for some expensive delays in the 1960s), the period of construction for the new fleet would be so long that reliance would have to be placed on a couple of *Polaris* boats beyond their expected life-span. What may well happen is that the construction of new attack submarines will be deferred to make way for the *Trident* submarines. This would immediately reduce the *net* cost to the budget and would have the bureaucratic advantage of making one group of submariners, rather than other service branches, pay for the good fortune of another group of submariners.

THE DEFENCE BUDGET

The eventual budgetary impact obviously depends on the extent to which defence expenditure contracts or expands in the future. This remains an open question. On the one hand the general state of the economy puts all public expenditure under pressure. On the other hand, the current Government insists that defence is a priority and that it hopes to fulfil the NATO norm of an annual 3 per cent rise in real terms in the defence budget.

The total defence budget, rather than its component parts, has become an object of political controversy over the past few years.

When the Labour Government came to power it was committed to a major review of the defence budget. The programme bequeathed to them would have resulted in a major expansion of the defence budget, ending in an expenditure by the end of the 1970s at a level almost 20 per cent higher than the eventual figure. The Defence Review of 1975 had as an objective the holding of the budget steady. It was hoped that if an economic growth rate of some 3 per cent was achieved then a stable defence budget would mean that the proportion of the nation's GNP assigned to defence would gradually decline (from 5.5 per cent to 4.5 per cent).

Unfortunately, the wretched economic performance of the 1970s not only made regular 3 per cent growth unobtainable, but put additional strain on all public expenditure. Defence spending was cut regularly, twice in 1975 and twice again in 1976. Thus the planned pre-Defence Review figure (at 1977 Survey prices) of £7436 million for 1977–8 was cut first to £6802 million in the Defence Review and then, by the later cuts, to £6329 million.

The savings required in the 1975 Defence Review were found by completing the contraction of Britain's non-European military effort. It judged the areas where Britain could make significant contributions to NATO as the Central Region, the Eastern Atlantic and Channel Areas, the security of the United Kingdom and its immediate approaches, the nuclear deterrent plus some specialist reinforcement capabilities. This left little room for further geographical contraction without seriously cutting the contribution to NATO in important, and politically sensitive, areas. When additional economies were required in 1975 and 1976, the Ministry of Defence preferred to reduce the quality of individual contributions, rather than the contributions themselves. The relevant forces had to make do with less manpower, training, equipment and supplies than might be considered necessary to maintain full combat effectiveness. It was a holding operation, maintaining a major NATO role for which sufficient funds were not available until economic conditions improved.

In 1976, with sterling sliding perilously for most of the year, the Prime Minister felt obliged to observe that without international financial assistance, the British might be unable to continue participating so fully in the defence of central Europe. Meanwhile, complaints were starting to be heard from the services that they were being asked to do far too much with far too few resources. In September 1977, Dr Joseph Luns, the Secretary General of NATO, wrote to the Defence Secretary Mr Mulley that: 'NATO, faced with an increasing threat, cannot afford any lessening of its members' defence efforts'; and that 'any further cuts by the United Kingdom would not be understood by its allies or find any measure of support on their part'.[2]

However, by this time the tide already appeared to have turned. In May 1977, Britain had agreed with the rest of the alliance to aim for annual real increases in the defence budget in the region of 3 per cent. The proviso was attached, largely for Britain's benefit, that 'for some individual countries economic circumstances will affect what can be achieved'.[3] But by this time Britain's economic position was improving, helped by North Sea oil. The Labour Government did implement the NATO increases even if this did only restore the budget to what had been planned in the 1975 Defence Review.

The Conservative Government took over in May 1979, pledged to make defence 'the first charge on our national resources', exempt from the drastic public expenditure cuts generally deemed essential. This pledge has thus far been fulfilled, though not without a challenge from ministers from other spending departments wishing to see the sacrifices shared. Moreover, the Government is finding that this regular rise means less than it seems. The problem is quite straightforward: 3 per cent is sufficient to maintain the existing defence effort but not to branch out into new types of activity. This is because of the high relative cost of each succeeding generation of military equipment, as well as the need to maintain highly skilled volunteer forces with competitive wages and salaries. The 3 per cent is needed to stand still. If the recent pay rises succeed in raising recruitment to make up for the shortfall in manpower then there will be a marked shift in the internal balance of the budget in this direction, away from equipment. Other areas identified for extra expenditure are air defences, the reserves, a new tank and a replacement for the *Jaguar* and *Harrier*, as well as the building up of basic stocks of ammunition and fuel.

It is unlikely that the funds necessary to maintain, let alone expand, the defence effort are going to be available throughout the 1980s. Historically, the level of defence expenditure has varied only slightly. Major shifts, upwards or downwards, have rarely been sustained for more than a few consecutive years. In the past, optimism on allocations to defence has been based on optimism on future economic performance. A new Government confident of its policies may plan on the basis of a long-term recovery, but the 1980s promises to be a difficult decade for all the economies of the West and there is as yet no evidence that the Government will be able to overcome the basic industrial faults that have held back growth for the past decades. In these circumstances, persistent rises in the defence budget will invite 'guns *versus* butter' types of controversy. As one well-informed Conservative backbencher has already commented: 'Unless the economy grows at a rate not experienced for a decade it may turn to be simply not a matter of doing less in defence than we have led people to believe, but even of some eventual reductions in the levels of planned expenditure'.[4]

It is in this context that the economic burden of a new nuclear force must be viewed. It will have an impact on planning when the search may well be on for ways of affecting major reductions in defence expenditure.

These turning points have been faced before in British defence policy. At regular intervals over the past three decades, reductions have had to be made because of budgetary pressures. Up to now the nuclear forces have been spared. In the mid-1950s, the Conservatives believed that greater dependence on nuclear power would permit substantial cuts in conventional forces. In the mid-1960s, the Labour Government could see no net financial benefits in not proceeding with *Polaris*, and eventually found its savings by withdrawing from East of Suez. In the mid-1970s another Labour Government cut through more geographical contraction, exempting *Polaris* because its upkeep was only a small charge on the budget. The next time the crunch comes, however, it is likely to be on the eve of major investment on the nuclear force.

Each component part of the defence budget has its own supporters, both domestic and international. If the gloomy but realistic economic prognosis for Britain in the 1980s is at all accurate then these supporters are destined to clash. *Trident* or an alternative successor force will become part of this debate and will give it a twist that was absent from the comparable debates in the 1970s, for it raises the questions of the proper balance between conventional and nuclear forces and the nature and extent of Britain's commitment to NATO. As the debate on defence priorities becomes more pointed, so the question on whether national nuclear forces have any useful role to play will require keener examination than ever before.

9 Arms Control

The prospect facing British Governments is that of political requirements for an expanding defence effort arising from a serious and tense international situation at a time when the requirements of domestic economic management point to constriction. One possible way out would be a period of serious detente, accompanied by equally serious arms control, which would calm East–West relations and allow both sides to reduce their force levels without a diminution of security.

That, at least, has been the theory. In the 1970s there was an attempt to put it to the test with the collection of conferences, negotiations and reciprocal gestures that came to be known as detente. The early results of this process were encouraging but it came to be jeopardised by disappointment in the West that little was being achieved by way of civil liberties in the Eastern bloc or in restraining Soviet adventurism in the Third World, combined with the intrinsic problems of negotiations on sensitive matters. The 1977–80 period, when *Polaris* replacement was developing as an issue, was characterised first by a sustained effort to achieve a series of arms-control agreements and then, after some apparent success with the June 1979 signing of the SALT II Treaty in Vienna, by a virtual collapse of these efforts. The Soviet invasion of Afghanistan, which marked the end of the 1970s, was followed by President Carter's request to the Senate to postpone ratification of SALT. Even before the invasion this ratification had been in doubt.

Even areas of comparative success indicate that at best arms control is a limited process, geared more to the management of arms competition, imposing some stability in certain areas, than radical disarmament. The achievements, such as they are, have tended to define the parameters of the arms competition (prohibiting deployment of nuclear weapons in outer space, Antarctica and Latin America and on the sea bed, prohibiting atmospheric testing of nuclear weapons and, indirectly, keeping the number of nuclear weapons states at five) rather than interfering with the dynamics of the competition.

This lack of success in arms control is relevant to British nuclear weapons policy, at least in the manner in which it has been presented in the past. It has been common to describe the British nuclear force as an unfortunate necessity in the absence of effective arms-control and disarmament treaties, and thus liable to substantial adjustment and even scrapping in the event of the successful conclusion of such treaties.

The lack of major steps towards disarmament has provided an argument against unilateral reductions. An illustration of this can be found in the movement of Labour policy through 1974. The position taken by the opposition party preparing to fight the March 1974 General Election was stated in the Manifesto as:

> We shall participate in the multilateral disarmament negotiations and as a first step will seek the removal of American *Polaris* bases from Great Britain.

Once in Government, this position had to be reformulated. It appeared in the manifesto for the October 1974 General Election as:

> Starting from the basis of the multilateral disarmament negotiations we will seek the removal of American *Polaris* bases from Britain.

This major proviso was extended to cover the *Polaris* force (as well as American bases) by Secretary of State for Defence Roy Mason. When asked in January 1975 when the *Polaris* force was to be phased out, Mr Mason replied:

> This will be subject to multilateral negotiations. We would like to get the Conference on Security and Cooperation in Europe and the MBFR negotiations out of the way first before we start talking about *Polaris* and its withdrawal.[1]

While Labour politicians have tended towards the view that the future of British nuclear forces is contingent upon the successful conclusion of disarmament treaties, Conservatives have been inclined to turn this round and argue that diplomatic achievements in this area depend on the bargaining strength that comes from possession of nuclear weapons.

Sir Alec Douglas-Home when Prime Minister used to claim that the nuclear force provided 'a ticket of admission' to a 'seat at the top table' at which Britain could exercise benign influence in pursuit of the common good as well as the national interest. That the existence of her own arsenal of nuclear weapons has provided Britain with a seat at the top table is not to be doubted. It was involved at every stage of the Partial Test Ban Treaty of 1963 and the Non-Proliferation Treaty of 1968; it sits alone with the Soviet Union and the United States in the current negotiations on a Comprehensive Test Ban Treaty (France and China have excluded themselves); participates actively in the talks on mutual and balanced force reduction in Europe (MBFR) and though not involved in the Strategic Arms Limitation Talks (SALT) has taken part in NATO consultations. Whether Britain exercises much influence while sitting at the top table is more open to doubt. Unless key decisions on Britain's nuclear forces are in some way subject to the outcome of arms-control deliberations its negotiating position is weak. In practice, as we shall now see, up to now arms control has been more of an influence upon, than an instrument of, British nuclear weapons policy. To demonstrate this point three negotiations will be examined in ascending order of importance. These are the Non-Proliferation Treaty (NPT), the Comprehensive Test Ban Talks (CTBT) and the Strategic Arms Limitation Talks (SALT).

NON-PROLIFERATION TREATY

There are a number of distinct approaches to non-proliferation. The most important is the Non-Proliferation Treaty, signed in 1968 (and which 106 states have now ratified), which in effect, limits the number of nuclear weapons states to five. Non-nuclear weapons states agree to stay that way in return for pledges from the nuclear-weapons states that they will work towards disarmament and make available the fruits of peaceful nuclear technology. Any nuclear facilities are provided only on condition of the application of safeguards arranged by the International Atomic Energy Agency (IAEA). There was a review conference of the NPT in May 1975 and there is to be another in September 1980. In order to strengthen the non-proliferation regime, the major suppliers of civilian nuclear technology have agreed on procedures for the transfer of nuclear technology which insist on the imposition of strict safeguards, even if the state in question has not ratified the NPT. The United States Congress has enacted legislation which goes further than these understandings. The problem is that there is no clear dividing line between military and civilian nuclear technologies and acquisition of the most sensitive civilian technologies, in particular reprocessing plants and enrichment facilities, can create the potential for an impressive military capability. The resultant difficulty is that attempts to interfere with the development and acquisition of the sensitive nuclear technologies can be perceived as an interference with peaceful trade and the creation of vital new energy supplies. Another, less technical, approach to non-proliferation is to rely on strategic common sense, emphasising the disincentives to proliferation (such as the possible loss of super-power support) and attempting to arrange nuclear-free zones around the globe. One such zone has been arranged in Latin America, which the British Government has agreed to honour, though there is not overwhelming confidence in its long-term viability.

Without entering into a detailed discussion of the proliferation problem, we can note that the menace is often exaggerated. India exploded a nuclear device in 1974, but is still a long way from developing a weapons capability. There still remain only five nuclear-weapons states, although Israel can be assumed to have a serious nuclear capability, which for obvious reasons it has chosen not to brag about. South Africa could be a nuclear-weapons state if it so desired. Pakistan has made little secret of its ambition to become a nuclear-weapons state during the early 1980s.

In general the most likely proliferators are 'pariah' states (Israel, South Africa, Taiwan and South Korea) and others who feel that a threatening regional power might 'go nuclear'. This focuses attention on the Middle East, the Indian sub-continent and Latin America (where regional rivalries may get the better of cooperative endeavours). In all of these cases proliferation could complicate conflicts that are already extremely difficult to resolve and a nuclear war, however much contained in some far-off region, could not but have major implications for all international activity. Nevertheless, it is extremely unlikely that any of these proliferators would have the means or the inclination to develop delivery vehicles that could attack targets in Britain (though a number of dependencies would be at risk). For example the People's Republic of China, which exploded its first nuclear bomb in 1964, has yet to deploy an ICBM capable of reaching Western Europe or the United States. Thus while an energetic nuclear non-proliferation policy makes sense for all sorts of foreign policy objectives, it is not essential for the purpose of preventing new nuclear threats to the United Kingdom. The major qualification to this point is that in the event of a break-up of NATO, most of Britain˜s current allies could 'go nuclear' without much difficulty.

Current non-proliferation efforts do not have a major impact on Britain's nuclear weapons programme. The most direct pressure is felt by Britain's civil nuclear programme: the development of the reprocessing facility at Windscale, has been criticised by the United States as contributing to the erosion of controls over sensitive nuclear technologies. There is a possibility that under the US Non-Proliferation Act a refusal by Europeans to allow their civilian nuclear programmes to be constrained by US norms, could result in a refusal to provide nuclear fuels in the future.

The only non-proliferation measure relevant to Britain's nuclear weapons programme is Article VI of the NPT:

> Each of the Parties to the Treaty undertakes to pursue negotiations in good faith on effective measures relating to cessation of the nuclear arms race at an early date and to nuclear disarmament, and on a treaty in general and complete disarmament under strict and effective international control.

As a commitment this is extremely weak. The obligation is attached to all parties and not just nuclear-weapons states. It is to pursue negotiations, but not to make them succeed (which is why the non-nuclear powers insisted on adding a clause which at least requires that the negotiations be pursued 'in good faith'). The immediate objectives are modest, requiring neither complete disarmament nor even a cessation of the arms race, but only 'effective measures relating to cessation of the nuclear arms race'.

There is therefore no binding obligation to do anything more than enter into arms-control negotiation with some serious intent.

The nuclear-weapons states presented the first SALT agreement as evidence of their good intentions, but with SALT II stuck in the US ratification process, and with little movement at the negotiations on a comprehensive test ban treaty and force reductions in Europe, there is an embarrassing lack of progress to show the non-nuclear-weapons states. Successful conclusion of these various negotiations would go some way towards calming the tempers of the non-nuclear-weapons states, particularly those which are also non-aligned, but it is unlikely that they will be fully satisfied until more radical measures are implemented.

There is no evidence that unilateral action by Britain, however drastic, will have anything other than a marginal effect on the attitudes and behaviour of non-nuclear weapons states. A move to increase significantly Britain's nuclear capabilities, rather than simply maintain them at existing levels, would generate some criticism and would serve to underline the value that the nuclear-weapons states continue to attach to their nuclear possessions. Nevertheless, a decision either way on the replacement of *Polaris* would make little difference to the success of the non-proliferation treaty and other non-proliferation strategies.

THE COMPREHENSIVE TEST BAN

In 1963 Britain joined with the United States and the Soviet Union and signed a Treaty prohibiting atmospheric tests of nuclear weapons. The result of this Treaty was to limit the incidence of a certain form of atmospheric pollution, but its effects on nuclear weapons development was slight as testing moved underground. Since 1963 there have been literally hundreds of underground nuclear tests. Only seven of these have been British, conducted at the American site at Nevada (Britain lacks her own facilities for testing).

In 1963 the parties to the Partial Test Ban Treaty agreed to seek 'the discontinuance of all test explosions of nuclear weapons for all time'. Progress towards this goal has been slow. In 1974 the United States and the Soviet Union signed an agreement to limit the yield of underground tests to 150 kilotons. Though this treaty was to take effect in March 1976 it has yet to be ratified by the US

Senate. This agreement was generally taken to be a cosmetic gesture, as most tests take place under the 150 kiloton theshold. In practice the United States has limited nuclear tests to the 100 kiloton range (a restriction that presumably is applied to British tests). In March 1977 the United States and the Soviet Union agreed to set up a working party to investigate the possibility of a comprehensive test ban treaty. In July 1977 the United Kingdom asked if it could join the discussions and this was agreed. There was little enthusiasm within the Ministry of Defence for this, but their doubts found no support among their own ministers who were part of a Government committed to arms control. It was pointed out that as Britain would be fully implicated, because of its dependence on American testing facilities, it might as well be involved.

Until the summer of 1978 there was good progress in the negotiations and Prime Minister James Callaghan felt able to inform the UN Special Session on Disarmament that an 'early agreement is within our grasp'. Since then it has slipped away, more because of arguments going on within the United States than disagreements with the Soviet Union. In a speech to the UN on 23 October 1978 Lord Goronwy-Roberts, Minister of State for Foreign and Commonwealth Affairs, noted that 'the complexities of the subject regrettably impose a limit on the speed of progress'. He stated British objectives as being a treaty 'which will be non-discriminatory in that it will ban nuclear explosions by all parties, nuclear and non-nuclear weapons states alike'. He stressed the need for adequate verification and for the 'widest possible adherence'. He added:

> Agreement in principle has been reached on many of the major issues in the negotiations, including the key point that the treaty should be genuinely comprehensive. The three negotiating parties are agreed that the treaty should ban all nuclear weapons tests in all environments and that peaceful nuclear explosions should be covered by a Protocol, which will be an integral part of the Treaty.

There has been virtually no information or comment upon the content of these important negotiations in the British press. Even by British standards this is quite remarkable. It is therefore necessary to illuminate the major issues by reference to the American debate which has been much more public.[2]

A Comprehensive Treaty would not prevent new weapons being developed, as laboratory experiments can tell scientists much of what they need to know and there is now some 30 years of experience to draw upon. However, they have not actually had to operate in this manner and so doubts remain about whether certain refinements to weapons could be introduced. Furthermore there would be some uncertainty over the reliability of the existing stockpile. A comprehensive ban could therefore slow down the advance of weapons technology and make any use of the weapons more risky, particularly a first strike. At issue is whether it would impair confidence in either side's ability to maintain a strong deterrent force. The major advantage claimed for such a Treaty is political – it would provide some extra evidence of the good faith of the nuclear powers in pursuing their side of the NPT bargain.

The problems connected with gaining agreement in this area have been three-fold. First, there was the perennial problem of verification. The techniques of seismic detection have now improved to the extent that there is general agreement on the ability to monitor all nuclear explosions above 5 kilotons. The second problem concerned the Soviet desire to be allowed the occasional peaceful nuclear explosions, ostensibly for such civilian purposes as digging reservoirs or diverting rivers, but potentially also for covert military purposes. It eventually agreed to a moratorium on such explosions for the duration of the Treaty.

The third issue was the desire to get as wide as possible support for a ban. The Soviet Union has in the past been reluctant to agree to putting brakes on its weapons development without comparable constraints on France and China. These two countries have consistently refused to go along with test bans, arguing that because of their late start with nuclear technology they are still catching up with the established nuclear powers. In these circumstances, the Russians will not agree to an indefinite ban. In the negotiations a ban of 3–5 years was discussed, with action after that depending, amongst other things, on the attitudes of France and China.

The British position under the Labour Government was to argue for a 5-year ban covering all explosions, with a firm commitment to further negotiations on making the prohibitions permanent. This was the American position too. In May 1978, President Carter decided to push for as comprehensive a treaty as possible, but his advisers underestimated the extent of internal opposition.

Leading the attack were the nuclear scientists, with the support of the Joint Chiefs of Staff and their Congressional fellow-travellers. They cast doubt on the verification procedures, demonstrating how, with some skilful (and risky) Soviet deception, tests up to 5 kilotons could be carried out without detection. They pointed out all the opportunities for improvements in weapons technology that might be forgone if no tests were permitted. More serious problems were raised concerning uncertainties as to the reliability of the existing stockpile. Nuclear weapons contain materials subject to deterioration. Without occasional 'proof tests' the condition of the stockpile would become open to doubt. Underlying all these objections was a sense that, if nuclear scientists were not allowed to test their devices now and again, their profession will lose much of its excitement and interest. Key scientists might drift away from the laboratories, reducing America's ability to maintain the technological capability to resume testing, should this become necessary.

It should be noted that a number of key scientists, including some of the former heads of US nuclear laboratories, disagreed with this opposition, arguing that it overestimated the possibilities of Soviet cheating, exaggerated the strategic gains that might come from such cheating, while overstating the problem of reliability.

It would not be surprising if British nuclear scientists displayed the same anxieties as some of their American colleagues. Indeed envoys from the American laboratories came over to Britain early in 1978 to see whether this was so. They appear to have received a sympathetic hearing. Dr Donald Kerr, a leading official connected with America's nuclear weapons programme, who managed to combine his post with fierce opposition to the Treaty, when asked on the views of the British noted a distinction between the Government's position and his technical counterparts in the Ministry of Defence and at Aldermaston:

> Their position is identical to ours on the technical issues of a CTB. This is very interesting on the face of it, in that two separate sets of technical people working independently have come up with the same technical positions. It gives you some faith that the physics is right, if nothing else is. I would say that technically we are in full agreement with our counterparts.[3]

However, there were some differences in the extent of the opposition. One of these was the difficulty the nuclear scientists had in interesting the British Chiefs of Staff in the campaign against the CTBT. Another was the fear that ministers were insufficiently committed to the future of the nuclear force to be too perturbed when told that its survival was incompatible with a CTBT.

Furthermore, as already indicated, much of the concern in the US is over the reliability of the existing stockpile, rather than obstacles to the development of new weapons. As the *Chevaline* programme has resulted in more up-to-date nuclear warheads, this is the most modern element of the *Polaris* force, and proof tests are not for the moment necessary. The fact that tests have been conducted during 1979, a year when it might have been hoped that a CTBT would have been in operation, indicates that it might have caused problems in the development of *Chevaline*. As the ban would have effect in the first instance for only 3 years, it need not interfere with a testing programme for the second half of the 1980s. Lastly, one should emphasise the weight of informed opinion that is convinced that both the reliability of existing warheads and the quality of future warheads can be guaranteed without testing.

Whatever the doubts of the British nuclear scientists, they made no impression on the Labour Government. By contrast, the Carter Administration began to waver. The US moved to a ban of only 3 years' duration. Though all tests would still be covered there was a strong hint to the military that testing would be resumed on the expiry of the Treaty. Officials in the Foreign Office were not pleased with this movement in the US position. They were aware of the scepticism amongst the non-nuclear powers of the nuclear powers' readiness to take arms control seriously, and it was feared that a watered-down version of a CTBT would be treated with derision.

James Callaghan, as Prime Minister, did his best to persuade President Carter to stick to his original position. He would have liked to have been able to present successful negotiations to the electorate to enhance his reputation as an international peacemaker. This was not to be.

By the time the Conservatives came to power in Britain the moment when a Treaty could have been signed had passed. It had become a matter of controversy in Washington and it could not be brought forward until SALT was ratified (an event now not likely until 1981 if at all). The US position was still to argue for a comprehensive ban, but now one of only 3 years' duration.

The official British position did not change with the new Government. The British suddenly found themselves the victim of a Soviet negotiating ploy. The Russians agreed to have 10 seismic detectors on their territory, but then started to insist on awkward conditions. One was that Soviet equipment must be used on Soviet territory. The veracity of any readings from Soviet equipment would not be trusted by suspicious Americans. Another condition was that America and Britain should also have 10 detectors on their territories. America agreed but Britain said this would be absurd because all its tests were carried out at the American test site at Nevada. Nor was the Government anxious to pay the installation cost of £3 million and running cost of £500,000 a year for each station. The Russians compromised by suggesting that the British stations should be scattered round the world in dependencies, some of which are no longer dependent. All Britain has offered is an existing site at Eskdalemuir. The new Government was quite unwilling to take this particular issue seriously.

The eagerness for a Treaty, characteristic of Mr Callaghan, has now subsided. There would be few tears in Whitehall if the exercise ground to a complete halt. Meanwhile, the Government attitude is characterised by a marked lack of interest.

SALT

The Strategic Arms Limitation Talks began in November 1969 between the United States and the Soviet Union. This was the first major arms control activity from which Britain had been excluded, but there does not seem to have been any suggestion that it should participate. The limitations discussed at SALT have been of two types: on defensive and on offensive arms.

We have already had cause to mention the SALT I Treaty on ABMs of which small nuclear powers have been considered to be the main beneficiaries, because of the reduced demands placed as a result on their offensive forces. (It remains the case, however, that Britain inaugurated the anti-ABM *Chevaline* programme after the Treaty.) The attempts to limit offensive arms have been less successful, because of complications introduced by the asymmetrical force structures of both sides and the steady advance of weapons technology during the course of the negotiations. The outlines for a treaty were agreed in November 1974, to supersede an interim agreement signed in May 1972. Unfortunately, for a variety of technical and political reasons, it proved difficult to turn this into a finished Treaty until June 1979.

The 1979 Treaty lasts until 1985 and consists of a ceiling of 2250 for all delivery vehicles (bombers, ICBMs and SLBMs) and a variety of sub-ceilings: 1320 for MIRVed missiles and bombers with cruise missiles; 1200 for MIRVed missiles; 820 for MIRVed ICBMs. There are some limits on testing of new missiles. A protocol to the treaty contains an agreement not to deploy mobile missiles or ground- and sea-launched cruise missiles until 1982 to allow time for further negotiations on these awkward matters. Because of the decline in political support for SALT in the US Senate, accelerated by the invasion of Afghanistan, the Treaty has yet to be ratified and probably will not be voted upon until 1981 at the earliest. For the moment the process has stagnated and its future is in doubt.

Although Britain is not involved directly in SALT it has had a continuing, rather negative, interest in the negotiations. This interest has been to ensure that the Americans did not agree to any measures that might interfere with Anglo-American strategic cooperation or that might actually implicate British forces in an agreement.

During SALT I negotiations the Soviet Union pressed the view that the British and French SLBMs ought to be considered in conjunction with US forces. In a unilateral statement in 1972, the Soviet delegation stated that:

> if during the period of effectiveness of the Agreement US allies in NATO should increase the number of their modern submarines to exceed the number of submarines they would have operational or under construction on the date of signature of the Agreement, the Soviet Union will have the right to a corresponding increase in the number of its submarines.

The United States did not accept this statement. Nor was there any visible Soviet fuss when the fifth French submarine was laid down in 1974. No extra Soviet submarines were permitted, and there was no pressure for a similar clause in SALT II.

A more difficult question has concerned the indirect effects of SALT. Ever since noting the restrictive non-transfer clause in the 1972 ABM Treaty, British officials had been worried that a future Treaty on offensive arms would contain comparable provisions that would be contravened in any Nassau-type deal. Other European allies were less concerned, so long as the SALT process was preoccupied with long-range ballistic missiles and bombers in which they had little interest. However, in 1975 a complicating factor was introduced with cruise missiles, which were thought to be so inexpensive and versatile as to be of value to NATO in a number of ways other than as a strategic weapon. Europeans could see possible uses of the cruise missile with conventional warheads, or supplementing those nuclear forces based in Europe which had hitherto been kept well out of SALT. They were anxious that these options be protected from SALT, if possible by keeping cruise missiles out of the Treaty, or at least ensuring that it was possible to transfer the know-how to the Europeans for them to produce their own cruise missiles.

In 1975 and 1976 pressure was put on the Ford Administration not to accept a restrictive clause on non-circumvention. A pledge to this effect was obtained. However, in 1977 alliance fears were revived. This was because the new Carter Administration decided to use air-launched cruise missiles (ALCMs) to give its B-52 bomber force a new lease of life, while simultaneously accepting in SALT that the ground- and sea-launched version (GLCMs and SLCMs) which were of more interest to Europeans should be severely restricted. European suspicions were roused when the Americans circulated a briefing paper on cruise missiles which stressed their disadvantages as well as advantages. The concern was that Washington was trying to convince the Europeans that, however valuable it might find cruise missiles, they were of little use in Europe and that the option could therefore be discarded without upset in SALT.

At a meeting of NATO's Nuclear Planning Group in October 1977, this fear over an American willingness to negotiate away the cruise missile option was given voice, as were apprehensions over the inevitable Soviet pressure to put obstacles in the way of transfers of military hardware and technology from the United States to Western Europe. The diplomatic shambles in 1978, as members of the alliance equivocated in attitude to the neutron bomb and then President Carter appeared to change his mind at the last minute, added to fears that the United States was not as prepared as before to look after European interests. The Americans, aware of these fears, began to exert themselves in an attempt to demonstrate convincingly that the opposite was the case.

In the negotiations the Soviet Union did propose a non-transfer clause which would involve a direct ban on the transfer of strategic missiles and 'components, technical descriptions and blueprints for the arms' to third parties. The United States resisted Soviet attempts to implicate third parties, but was unable to actually claim a right to circumvent the Treaty. Article XII of the 1979 Treaty states: 'In order to ensure the viability and effectiveness of this Treaty, each party undertakes not to circumvent the provisions of this Treaty, through any other state or states, or in any other manner.' In unilateral statements the Americans have insisted that while it will not blatantly circumvent any Treaty, it will not allow any interference with normal patterns of cooperation with its allies, which of course includes a substantial and regular amount of technology transfer. As many of the key technologies are relevant to a number of systems, any attempt to impose rigid controls would do immense damage to alliance relationships. For Britain, this formulation opens the way to a new missile deal with the United States, presented as being in furtherance of the 1963 Polaris Sales Agreement.

During the negotiations Carter Administration officials became rather irritated at the extent to which Europeans refused to accept their word on how they were firmly resisting Soviet demands for a non-transfer clause, but instead wanted detailed assurances. If anything they found the German position most annoying because it was to protect options – conventionally armed cruise missiles – that they were unlikely ever to want to exercise. However, it was the British who were most persistent. When the British Aerospace studies suggested that a super-sonic cruise missile might be an appropriate course for Britain, assurances were required that this would not be closed by SALT (the Americans considered this a matter for SALT III). When the British were considering the advisability of a cruise missile for either *Vulcan* or *Tornado* aircraft they became concerned that this might be ruled out until 1985, because this might put the air-launched cruise missiles available to the West above the SALT limits. Although Britain was not to be a party to SALT would it be under pressure to conform with its provisions?

The British officials involved were not acting to support an agreed weapons programme, but the options they were seeking to preserve had not been ruled out and they felt it to be their duty to ensure that they were not lost by default. In the event they were relieved to have so many written assurances from the Americans when the Conservatives came to office in May 1979. Mrs Thatcher was suspicious of SALT, having been influenced by some of the more hawkish opponents of SALT in the United States. The Conservative election manifesto suggested (without explanation) that the British deterrent was more necessary than ever because of SALT. The main concern was with non-transfer provisions and once Mrs Thatcher could be convinced that there was no problem here, she was prepared to endorse SALT publicly. This she did the week after the election. The conversion required some persuasion and even then she was only prepared (for a while) to support the fact of agreement between the super-powers, as they had put so much effort into the negotiations, rather than the actual contents of the Treaty.

The definite American assurances on this matter then presented an opportunity to Britain. In order to secure acceptance of SALT, the Carter Administration had become so anxious to demonstrate both to NATO and the US that relations with allies would not be impaired, that it was in no position to refuse a reasonable request for the transfer of technology. Indeed, so anxious did President Carter become to undermine the position of his critics that officials in his Administration were almost inviting requests. This paved the way for sympathetic response to British queries about the possibility of purchasing *Trident*.

10   The Strategic Context

The various technological, industrial and economic factors which we have described push Britain towards a continuity in capabilities: a small but survivable submarine force, with ballistic missiles most suitable for attacks on major centres of industry and population. It is true that the warheads likely to come with *Trident* will split into a large number of very accurate warheads, permitting attacks on some highly protected military targets, but not enough to create a 'counter-force' option of any seriousness. As before, the new system will depend on the goodwill of the United States.

Since 1962 when the type of force described above was first adopted, Britain's strategic position has changed. It is no longer the self-evident 'second in command in the West', and it has confirmed the regional bias in its foreign policy, not only by concentrating its military effort in Europe but also by joining the European Communities. NATO remains at the centre of Britain's security policy. The alliance itself has demonstrated impressive permanence, but within it West Germany is now fully rehabilitated and has become once again the strongest classical military power in Europe, while France has withdrawn from the integrated military command.

Meanwhile, the doubts that were strong in the 1960s over the US nuclear guarantee to Europe, after subsiding for a while, have gradually come to the fore once again, prompted by the impressive growth in all Soviet military capabilities, one of the most prominent features of the period since 1962 (the year of the Cuban Missile Crisis as well as the Nassau Agreement). This has led to a discussion within NATO of a variety of measures for making the US guarantee more plausible, some of which have been implemented. One consequence is a return of the nuclear bias in

NATO deliberations, and this affects both Britain's view of its own nuclear capabilities and the attitudes of its allies to these capabilities.

NUCLEAR WEAPONS AND NATO

There is a basic difference between the two alliances of NATO and the Warsaw Pact which has enormous political and military consequences: whereas the members of the Warsaw Pact are grouped reasonably closely together, huddled around the dominant military power, those of NATO are widely dispersed, with the dominant military power separated from all but one of the others by a large ocean. The result of this is that NATO's strongest military cards are not located at the point where Soviet power is at its most imposing.

The political problem this creates is the inevitable doubt over whether the United States shares the same interest in countering Soviet power as its allies, given that it is in no danger of invasion and occupation. The military problem this creates is in transporting American military power across the Atlantic Ocean in an emergency to bolster NATO's defences. The mobilisation of American reserve forces and their safe delivery to Europe is the major preoccupation of NATO's conventional military planning. But with 'strategic' nuclear weapons, that is those aimed at targets in the enemy's homeland, vital to its viability as a modern industrial and military power, the problem does not exist. The long range of modern missiles means that the Soviet Union and all other important Warsaw Pact countries can be easily reached from missiles and aircraft based in the United States. Consequently, NATO's most important strategic assets can reside on one side of the Atlantic Ocean while on the other side are those members most at risk, nervous that an attack upon them will not be deemed, in Washington, a sufficient threat to Europe to warrant the activation of its nuclear arsenal.

When nuclear protection was first offered to Europe, the United States enjoyed a nuclear monopoly. As soon as the Soviet Union became able to launch a nuclear attack of any magnitude on the United States scepticism inevitably surrounded its promises to Europe. It took no great political insight to realise that an American President would think hard and long before unleashing his nuclear forces on behalf of Europe if this was likely to result in national suicide.

In the late 1950s and early 1960s this loss of credibility caused great dismay. The French, in particular, made no secret of their view that the US nuclear umbrella was now so full of holes that it had become worse than useless. Yet it was only the French who actually re-oriented their strategy to take account of this new development. The other allies preferred to believe in the guarantee, as an act of faith, on the positive grounds that it still had sufficient credibility to pose unacceptable risks to the Soviet Union, and on the more negative grounds of a lack of serious alternatives and a probability that the guarantee would never, anyway, be put to the test.

The Soviet retaliatory capability made it unlikely that the United States would engage in a nuclear war except in the most extreme of circumstances; little could be done by way of new military capabilities to alter this. The response within NATO was to ensure that the United States felt that any attack on its allies constituted the 'most extreme of circumstances'. To achieve this there have been regular acts of mutual re-assurance: the United States insists that its commitment to European security is firm and robust, and the Europeans have insisted that they believe this. To add credibility to these assurances a complex symbolism has developed, based on deployments of military forces.

The term used in NATO to describe anything that might break the vital link between the two continents of Europe and North America is 'de-coupling'. The term is awkward, not only because the proper English is *un*-coupling, but also because the real NATO problem is 'coupling', that is holding together countries that share key political and economic interests, but which do diverge in narrow strategic interests – varying in geographical position, proximity to the threat, vulnerabilities and strengths.

The real strength of the alliance depends on a sense of common identity and shared interests: that the close economic, political and cultural ties introduced a sense of belonging to a single Atlantic community. Whatever the short-term temptations to remain isolated from a European crisis, the United States could not tolerate the domination of Europe by a single power. The alliance could be threatened by any developments that disrupt its unity, including arguments over economics and energy, as well as those confined to the military sphere, but this also means that it is held together by much more than crude calculations of military power. This is in contrast to the view that the state of the central strategic balance between the two super-powers determines the quality of the alliance bond: that comparative strategic advantage (or at least the perception of such) determines the readiness of the United States to offer, and the Europeans to trust, a nuclear guarantee.

The symbolism surrounding the coupling of America to Europe is largely connected with the basing of American forces in Europe. It has become accepted that these forces are as important as an earnest of American commitment to the defence of Europe than for their intrinsic military worth. Hints of large-scale reductions in force levels have been greeted with European horror as if less men on the ground represented a slackening of the American commitment.

To complicate matters further, this has not meant that extra forces have been unreservedly welcomed. A danger has also been seen in encouraging a different sort of 'de-coupling' by basing sufficient forces in Europe to allow for a continental war which left North America untouched. This might suggest that a war could be conducted in Europe in a manner most convenient to the United States irrespective of whether, by being bloody, confined and drawn out, it suited the Europeans. Furthermore, it has been believed that the core of NATO's deterrent is America's strategic forces. The impression that all European crisis could be brought to a successful conclusion without the invocation of these strategic forces has been considered not only erroneous, but actually harmful to NATO solidarity.

The doctrine of flexible response as adopted by NATO in 1967 does not assume that there is any self-evident means of defeating a determined Soviet assault on Europe. It is best understood as a preparation for a process of escalation which has two distinct and not necessarily complementary objectives. The first is to contain any conflict at as low a level of violence as possible for the length of time necessary to allow for a negotiated settlement; the second is to indicate a readiness to raise the level of violence if the West's position is deteriorating, threatening not so much to retrieve lost ground but to make the enemy pay more dearly for any gains he has made. Escalation is a difficult concept because it suggests both a deliberate effort to control war and the possibility that it might all get terribly out of control. The threat of uncontrollable violence operates as a deterrent to war; the promise of a modicum of control offers a way out if deterrence should fail.

The major escalatory move in a war would be to start it in the first place. Then it would be to move from conventional to nuclear weapons. For this reason the strategy requires serious conventional forces. While Europeans have yet to accept an American definition of 'limited war' as one confined to Europe, they have come to agree that a policy based wholly on nuclear deterrence without some conventional options lacks credibility and would leave NATO handicapped in an emergency. One of the virtues of greater conventional strength is therefore in raising the threshold – putting back the awful moment of the resort to nuclear weapons. In this way a decline in conventional forces creates more and more reliance on the deterrent effects of nuclear weapons.

It is a matter of some dispute whether there are any clear rungs in the escalation ladder once the nuclear threshold has been passed. NATO strategy assumes that the incentives for restraint would still apply even after the first nuclear volleys. Others, including many Soviet strategists, assume that this would be the signal for all-out nuclear exchanges. With a vivid (and morbid) imagination many nuclear rungs in the escalation ladder can be suggested, but four basic ones figure prominently in Western strategic studies: short-range, battlefield theatre nuclear forces; long-range, interdiction theatre nuclear forces; counter-force strategic nuclear forces; counter-city strategic nuclear forces.

In the late 1970s much attention was devoted to the state of the strategic balance, as if the imminence of some decisive Soviet superiority was a fact of contemporary international life. If so, then the foundation of NATO's whole strategy would be at risk, because the Soviet Union could contemplate a move up the escalation ladder with greater equanimity than the United States. However, careful examination of the strategic balance reveals that the proposition of growing Soviet superiority is dubious.

PARITY OR SUPERIORITY

In the mid-1960s the Soviet Union began a major build-up in all areas of military power that has continued, with only occasional pauses, ever since. In strategic arms the impression of dramatic movement was accentuated by the apparent passivity in the

United States. However, it was only the absolute levels of American forces that were stagnant. More new missiles were produced in the United States than in the Soviet Union. The difference was that whereas the United States removed old missiles to make way for the new, the Russians could not bring themselves to discard perfectly adequate old missiles, so they added to their totals.

To assess the current situation a good starting point is the figures on super-power forces both sides agreed at the time of the SALT II Treaty in June 1979. These figures show that the Soviet Union has more ICBMs than the United States (1398 as against 1054) and more which can carry MIRVs (608 as against 550). While the accuracy of the US warheads remains greater than those of the Soviet Union, this gap has been narrowed and is more than compensated for by the Soviet advantages in size – the average Soviet ICBM carries far more warheads of larger yield than the average American ICBM. The Americans are upgrading the warheads of their ICBMs, but the next generation (known for the moment as M-X) will not start to become available until 1986 at the earliest. Meanwhile, the Soviet programme of ICBM modernisation still has considerable momentum behind it. By about 1982 it is expected that, by using only about a quarter of its total ICBMs in a surprise attack, the Soviet Union would be able to destroy all but a few of the American ICBMs, plus all SLBMs at port and heavy bombers that have been unable to fly from their bases. In addition, there have been reports of a number of follow-on Soviet ICBMs still under development.

The figures of SLBMs show the Soviet Union ahead on overall numbers (950 as against 656) but still, in this category, well behind the US on MIRVed SLBMs (144 as against 496). The warhead package carried in US SLBMs is also much more sophisticated. However, the major US advantages lie with the submarines themselves, with boats of more advanced design; less noisy and, in consequence, less vulnerable to anti-submarine warfare techniques (in which the United States is also well ahead). In addition, the Soviet boats have fewer ports, none of which is particularly easy to leave, because of weather conditions or the boats' conspicuity to NATO's submarine patrols. Reports suggest that only about one-fifth or less of these boats are on station at any one time, which means that those stuck in port are extremely vulnerable to an American surprise attack. (The Americans keep about half of their boats on station.) Finally, while the Russians have been investing funds in an effort to improve their capabilities, this is an area where the Americans are engaged in an active (and extremely expensive) modernisation programme. The new *Trident* I SLBM is now being delivered to the US Navy and next year the first of the *Trident* submarines will become available. By the late 1980s another new SLBM (*Trident* II) should be fully developed and ready for production.

On the figures for heavy bombers, the United States is shown up as being well ahead (573 as against 156). However, 224 of the US B-52 bombers are in storage and a certain discount should be made to take account of the fact that US bombers have to penetrate significant air defences while Soviet bombers face no such obstacles. Nevertheless, this is still an area of major US advantage. The heavy bombers owned by both sides are based on 1950s models and so are tending towards obsolescence. There has been an argument in the United States over whether the Soviet *Backfire* bomber has any intercontinental role. As this would be an extremely difficult and inefficient way of using this aircraft, it can be assumed that it is only designed for operation in the European theatre. There have been reports, as yet unconfirmed, of three new Soviet long-range bombers in development. The United States has developed one new bomber, the B-1, but has decided against putting it into production, preferring to extend the active life of the B-52, by converting it to carry air-launched cruise missiles (ALCMs).

To sum up it can be seen that US strategic assets are more evenly spread among ICBMs, SLBMs and bombers than those of the Soviet Union, which has a force structure dominated by ICBMs. To illustrate this, we can compare equivalent megatonnage (EMT), a measure of the capacity to destroy 'soft' targets such as cities. The ICBM force provides less than 25 per cent of total US EMT, but 75 per cent of Soviet EMT. The other point is that, independently of SALT, the balance will be seen (in terms of number of warheads and vulnerability of hard targets, such as ICBMs, to surprise attack) to be shifting towards the Soviet Union during the first half of the 1980s, and then can be expected to shift back towards the United States during the second half.

The current gloom over the strategic balance results solely from attributing excessive consequences to the developing Soviet advantages in ICBMs. The scenario is one of a Soviet surprise attack wholly destroying the US ICBM force, but using only a small number of its own missiles, held in reserve for further volleys. As ICBMs are the only weapons accurate enough to attack other ICBMs, the United States would then be unable to mount a comparable counter-force attack and, with its cities held hostage, unwilling to escalate by staging a counter-city attack. The mere thought of this eventuality, it is suggested, would paralyse a US President and make him subject to the most malevolent blackmail.

This scenario is overdrawn. A surprise first strike against US ICBMs with untested weapons would be a considerable risk. Soviet planners could neither be sure that the United States would not launch its ICBMs on warning of impending attack nor that, despite the escalatory consequences, it would not retaliate with bombers and SLBMs. The major fallacy is to assume that a Soviet attack against US ICBMs would be experienced as a limited attack on solely military targets. In fact, ten million or more US citizens would be killed, sufficient to be considered a counter-population attack deserving of a full retaliation.

To the extent that there is a problem here, it is associated with the first half of the 1980s, before the new mobile ICBM, M-X, will become operational. Even with M-X the essential problem of the US nuclear guarantee will remain. It is not a new problem, based on recent trends in weapons' programmes, but a well-established consequence of the development of a Soviet retaliatory capability that would make any US nuclear use potentially suicidal.

THEATRE NUCLEAR FORCES

Apart from affirmations of the common NATO interest, one way to ease this problem has been found with the deployment of US nuclear forces within Europe. To Europeans the advantage of this arrangement is that it links the American nuclear weapons to the defence of the continent. The military advantages have always been less clear because of the problem of using these weapons to good effect without destroying those being defended.

The two categories of theatre nuclear forces (TNF) are the short-range, which are for battlefield use, and the long-range, which are to attack enemy supply lines and reserves. Short-range TNF were recently surrounded with much controversy with regard to the neutron bomb, which will be examined briefly in the next chapter. For the moment it is long-range TNF that are most directly relevant for British nuclear weapons policy.

For many years these weapons appeared of only slight relevance to the dominant themes of contemporary strategic analysis – a US–USSR nuclear exchange or a Warsaw Pact attempt to breach NATO's defences – and to the two arms control negotiations – SALT and MFBR – which reflected these dominant themes. The 'grey area' was identified as comprising those nuclear weapons that had somehow been neglected and ignored in the past.

The starting point for our examination is the Soviet capability in this area. Whereas the geographical dispersion of NATO is a great weakness, the concentration of the Warsaw Pact is a great strength. All the forces needed to fight a land war in Europe are close at hand. However, to be able to mount nuclear attacks against all its potential enemies, the Soviet Union needs weapons of quite distinct ranges – some to cover the comparatively short distances to Western Europe and China, and some to stretch out over the Atlantic Ocean to the United States.

Because the European part of NATO is easier to reach, Soviet nuclear capabilities were developed against it first. During the 1950s medium-range bombers and then missiles were introduced. In the latter category came two missiles – the medium-range SS-4 and the intermediate-range SS-5 – of which over 700 became operational from the late 1950s to 1964. In the West this deployment was commonly viewed as a 'quick-fix' to the Soviet predicament of facing a direct US nuclear threat without being able to reply fully in kind. Western Europe was made 'hostage' to American good behaviour while the Kremlin waited for a proper intercontinental capability to be assembled. Once this capability was in place, it was assumed that the SS-4s and SS-5s had become redundant. They were too clumsy and inaccurate to support other combat operations. Furthermore, as the societies of Western Europe were presumed to be the prize for which the Soviet Union might go to war, there was every incentive for it to avoid destroying this prize in an undiscriminating nuclear attack. The continued presence of these missiles was a consequence of the Soviet disinclination to remove any established weapons in working order, however superfluous to requirements.

This perception of Soviet theatre forces underestimated the extent to which the Soviet Union has felt it necessary to be able to target all of its major opponents (including China) and probably overestimated the extent to which it was willing to pull any punches to spare Western Europe in the event of a war. The Russians have always expected to use their nuclear forces against military targets, on the grounds that even a nuclear war was to be 'won' in some sense. An important collection of these military targets are based in Western Europe. However, they have shown little interest in Western ideas of limited war in which every effort is made to avoid collateral damage to civilians unfortunate enough to be living near military installations. The only 'limited war' of interest to the Russians is one that leaves them untouched.

In the late 1960s a new factor emerged in Soviet calculations – the deepening split with its former ally, the People's Republic of China. This provided a new set of targets for medium and intermediate range missiles. In 1968 about a quarter of the Soviet arsenal was moved to positions facing the Far East.

A visible reminder of the Soviet interest in weapons of this range came in the early 1970s, first with a new bomber – the *Backfire* – and then with a new intermediate range ballistic missile (IRBM) – the SS-20. The SS-20 was not the first attempt to develop a replacement for the older missiles. An earlier attempt had ended in failure in the late 1960s and then a number of ICBMs had been assigned to European targets as a temporary expedient. One of the causes of delay was difficulty with solid-fuel technology, necessary for a missile to be launched quickly. The SS-20 was a spin-off from the development of the SS-16 ICBM, itself an unsuccessful programme. The SS-20 is far superior in range, speed of launch and accuracy than its predecessors, and it has a MIRVed warhead. It is estimated that some 250 SS-20s will be operational by the mid-1980s, of which about two-thirds will be facing Western Europe.

Over time, Britain became the only European country involved in providing a response to this particular Soviet threat, both with its own forces, and as a host to those of the United States. The only other Euopean nuclear power, France, does not assign its forces to NATO, while the American IRBMs, *Thor* and *Jupiter*, which had been based in Italy and Turkey as well as Britain, were removed in the early 1960s. The collapse of proposals for a multilateral force meant that NATO's long-range theatre forces consisted only of American aircraft based in Britain and on aircraft carriers patrolling European waters, a portion of American SLBMs (400

Poseidon warheads) and the British *Polaris* SLBMs and *Vulcan* aircraft.

The sea-based component was not considered wholly suitable for the role normally attributed to theatre forces – attacks on urgent, militarily relevant targets to the rear of the front line. SLBMs are not accurate and do not lend themselves to subtle variations in attacks. For example, the danger of revealing the position of the carrying submarines makes it unwise to launch just a couple of missiles at a time. In addition, the American SLBMs are so linked with all the other central strategic systems that the distinctiveness of a response involving them might have been lost both on enemies and allies. As for the British *Polaris* fleet, while the Americans have habitually classified it as part of NATO's theatre forces, Britain has described it officially as a strategic force. *Polaris* has been seen more as a last-resort deterrent than something to be introduced early on in a process of nuclear escalation.

Thus the pre-eminent theatre nuclear forces have been aircraft, currently 170 American F-111s and 56 British *Vulcans*, all based in England. The problem with these aircraft lies with their age; their vulnerability to surprise attack, which includes a dependence on long concrete runways; and their difficulties in penetrating Soviet air defences.

At some point the question of the modernisation of these forces would have had to be faced. It was eventually raised in the first half of 1977 when the new Carter Administration in the United States was drawing up a plan for a Long-Term Defence Programme, which was launched at the London NATO Summit of May 1977. One question asked was whether some of NATO's nuclear systems threatening the Soviet homeland actually needed to be based in Europe or whether systems off-shore, either in submarines or in aircraft carriers, would suffice. This matter of TNF modernisation was designated as one of the ten fields for priority study and action in the plan. The responsibility for the study was given to the Nuclear Planning Group which, in October 1977, set up a working group, known as Task Force 10 and later as the High-Level Group, to do the job.

By the time it got down to work the issue was no longer one of modernising specific components of NATO's forces. It had become complicated by two significant trends in NATO's strategic thought.

The first of these trends was an exploration of the possibilities for limited and controlled forms of nuclear attacks. The exploration was prompted first by concern that by concentrating on all-out, city-busting nuclear exchanges, NATO may have locked itself into a strategy that admitted of no possibility but mutual suicide once nuclear weapons were introduced into an East–West conflict; and second by optimism over the potential of new technologies, particularly those of precision guidance, as a source of alternative strategies. These would involve discrete and discriminating strikes against targets chosen to demonstrate seriousness of purpose or to weaken the enemy's military position rather than destroy civilian life.

One influential concept was that of 'escalation dominance', by which strategic advantage goes to that side which can escalate with greatest ease (always accepting some unavoidable risk of a full-blooded retaliation). The concern over ICBM vulnerability discussed earlier (see pp. 107-8) reflects this theory and it also influences perceptions of the Soviet SS-20. According to this view the counter-force capability is the SS-20's most dangerous property for it could allow an attack on NATO's air bases and nuclear stockpiles, thus eliminating the alliance's ability to respond in kind. The only response left would require the introduction of US central strategic systems – a difficult and dangerous process of escalation. If nuclear war is to have any semblance of deliberate direction this may well be the form it would take, though it is difficult to have confidence that each move up the escalation ladder could be modulated with the proper care or would be received as intended, or that a means could be found to call a halt once some threshold had been reached.

The second important trend in NATO was a contemplation of the implications of visible strategic parity between the superpowers, achieved by the Soviet Union after a determined build-up and consolidated with some rigidity in SALT. As symmetry was seen to be achieved at the highest level, attention has been directed to military asymmetries lower down the line.

Politicians found the SS-20 handy in returning Soviet propaganda, using this missile to demonstrate that the Russians had hardly been laggards in improving their own capabilities. The defence specialists became unhappy with the tendency to present NATO's own moves towards improving its nuclear forces as merely a response to Soviet moves. The case for this modernisation stood on its own merits because of real strategic needs, they insisted, irrespective of any Soviet activity. They became anxious lest a serious concession by the Soviet Union on its own SS-20s would put the NATO programme in jeopardy.

The potential problems here were accentuated by long-range theatre weapons coming to be tangled up in SALT. At the start of SALT, the Americans, at the urging of their allies, had kept these systems out of the negotiations, but now they were being drawn in. First, the Americans became worried how Soviet theatre systems might be used against them, with some mid-air re-fuelling for the *Backfire* bomber or an extra stage on the SS-20, and began to demand assurances that these weapons were solely for theatre use, a matter of slight comfort to Europeans. Then, and more seriously, American cruise missiles got caught in the SALT net. One of the weapons covered by the protocol to the Treaty was the ground-launched cruise missile, a prime candidate for NATO's TNF modernisation. When the draft contents of the protocol became known in October 1977, there was some dismay, both in the United States and Europe, with critics arguing that any provisions of the protocol were likely to be carried over after its formal expiry.

Pressures built up around President Carter, to insist that the United States would not be bound by the dictates of the protocol more than was strictly necessary and then to go out of his way to prove that this was so by authorising production of those weapons the protocol mentioned. The entanglement of theatre systems with SALT, and the timetable imposed by the negotiations, forced not only the United States but also its allies to clarify their interests in these systems and the preferred approaches to their modernisation. The manner in which this was done illustrates the political complexities surrounding contemporary nuclear decision-making within Europe.

11 Nuclear Politics in Europe

The decision-making on the long-range theatre nuclear weapons in 1979 was very much influenced by the experience of the previous 2 years with the 'neutron bomb'.

THE NEUTRON BOMB

Neutron bombs or 'enhanced radiation weapons' emphasise one form of lethal effect from nuclear explosions – prompt radiation – while playing down other effects – blast, heat and fallout. They were designed for use against tanks, as neutron or gamma rays are able to penetrate tank armour and disable the crew. Warheads of this sort have been under discussion in NATO since 1974 in connection with two systems, the *Lance* short-range ballistic missile and an 8-inch artillery shell. They were to be used in the forces of Western European countries, including Britain, controlled as with other theatre nuclear weapons by a double-key system with the United States. These have been controversial weapons. At first their functions and capabilities were misunderstood as being intended for use against cities, where they would 'kill people but leave property intact'. In fact the explosion of one of these weapons would cause something more than minor subsidence. A more considered objection was that the temptation to use them against a Soviet invasion could trigger prematurely an all-out nuclear war in Europe. Supporters of the bomb have felt that its capabilities against tanks, and the limited collateral damage associated with its use, will indeed make it easier to use, so making deterrence more credible. This debate illustrated the general problem of how strengthening deterrence may involve running greater risks of nuclear war. However, neutron bombs are far more similar to existing tactical nuclear weapons than either their proponents or opponents have acknowledged, and that therefore the practical consequences for NATO's military position, if deployed, would be limited.

Whatever the actual merits or demerits of the weapon it acquired a reputation of being uniquely pernicious and the question of its deployment caused immense political awkwardness within NATO.

The alliance debate was reminiscent in its confusion of the great days of the Multilateral Force of the early 1960s. It began with a leak in the American press in 1977 that a new and pernicious weapon was to be introduced into NATO's arsenal. The ministers of NATO countries were unprepared for the rush of publicity and unacquainted with the weapon or the doctrine supporting it. They therefore prevaricated.

No government was prepared to accept responsibility for giving the 'go-ahead'. The United States was saying: 'We will deploy if you in Europe, where it will be deployed, declare in public that you actually require it'; meanwhile the Europeans were saying: 'Mr President this is your decision as your money is to be spent on production. We will accept it if you produce it'. There was thus monumental buck-passing back and forwards across the Atlantic. Eventually by early 1978 a sort of consensus was reached in which it was agreed that the Americans would begin production but deployment could be avoided and evidence of a slowing down of new weapons deployment, including the SS-20, by the Soviet Union, over a 2-year period.

At some point in March 1978 it seems that President Carter became disturbed that his officals were arranging an excessively pro-neutron bomb consensus. He had spoken often about his dislike for nuclear weapons, he was to be responsible for production of these weapons yet he was to authorise production without positive support from the Europeans. The Europeans meanwhile had been definitely, but slowly, preparing the ground for a production decision. Then overnight the signals from Washington were reversed: they were informed that President Carter, without seeking any advice from his own staff, had decided that there was to be no production. Herr Genscher, the German

Foreign Minister, flew to Washington and the decision was altered once again, to deferral of a final decision on production in case future Soviet activity justified yet another reversal. Rather than agree on whether this weapon is or is not a useful addition to the Western arsenal it was instead placed in a crude and implausible role as a diplomatic bargaining chip between East and West.

The lessons to be drawn from the neutron bomb episode were political more than military. The undistinguished character of the debate over its strategic consequences was in itself an important political fact. The complex issues of nuclear deterrence at the European level had not received a proper airing for over a decade, and there were indications that Europe's political leaders were as mystified by it all as their electorates. So long as these issues did not become matters of political controversy their resolution could be left to those who did understand what was going on: mainly officials in the defence ministries of the larger NATO members. However, once controversy was introduced, affecting alliance countries in a variety of ways, the mechanisms for collective decision-making appeared quite inadequate.

Any proposed adjustment to NATO's nuclear arsenal now seemed destined to spark off controversy. The Soviet Union was determined not to let NATO be strengthened in any significant manner without a serious protest. The propaganda campaign of the sort the Russians mounted on the neutron bomb ought not to have been so surprising. They have always been touchy on the subject of nuclear weapons based in Europe: campaigns were waged before against the Multilateral Force and any hints of German access to nuclear weapons. They pressed for the inclusion of American aircraft based in Europe capable of attacking Soviet territory in SALT. The major novelty in the Soviet neutron bomb campaign of 1977–8 was its sustained intensity, plus the fact of its sympathetic reception in some European countries. Protest over the neutron bomb was by no means confined to left-wing circles (where it was certainly strong). A number of religious groups found the weapon offensive, and their repugnance found resonance in a substantial segment of public opinion. The phenomenon was most notable in Holland, but it had strong expression in West Germany as well as in Scandinavia where there was an established opposition to anything connected with nuclear power, civilian or military. The re-activation of the anti-nuclear weapons constituency in Europe, long dormant, meant that any improvement to NATO's nuclear forces would have to anticipate serious opposition.

The debate in West Germany on the neutron bomb exposed something of that country's peculiar strategic predicament. By its proximity to the Warsaw Pact is has the keenest interest both in a sturdy defence and stable relations with the East. Having the most to lose in any war, it required the most imposing of nuclear deterrents to be operated on its behalf, yet would suffer enormously if the deterrent forces ever had to be activated. To a German the most 'tactical' of nuclear weapons is strategic in its local consequences. Finally, having recovered all of its economic and much of its political power after the war, it does not feel completely rehabilitated and is nervous over the reactions of its neighbours if it throws its considerable weight around in pursuit of its own self-interest.

The Germans developed a stake in NATO in which the United States took a determined lead, being made aware of European interests through regular consultation. European interests largely took the form of resisting any attempts at any major adjustments to the American force structure that implied a reassessment of the commitment to Europe, while discovering just how much they had to do themselves to keep the Americans happy that their allies were doing 'their bit'. Now President Carter, in the belief that he was responding to a European desire for increased consultation, was drawing the allies into responsibility for taking some of the difficult decisions. The Americans presumed the Europeans could look after their own interests, and would not, as in the past, feel obliged to anticipate their interests for them.

THEATRE NUCLEAR MODERNISATION

This experience provided the unpromising background to the developing debate on long-range theatre nuclear forces (TNFs), which was following close behind that on short-range nuclear forces. The expressions of dismay over President Carter's handling of the neutron bomb decision meant that his Administration was anxious to be more considerate of alliance feelings next time round. Unfortunately the signals it was receiving from Western Europe were ambiguous. The persistent questioning as to non-transfer clauses in SALT betrayed an interest in a cruise missile

option without clear evidence that thought had been given to
what sort of option and whether it should be exercised. Attention
focused mainly on West Germany. The Germans had been most
visibly unhappy over the neutron bomb episode, and were worry-
ing most in public over the SS-20 and the quality of American
leadership in NATO. There were therefore many in Washington
anxious to provide comfort and reassurance in any way the
Germans required. The political sensitivity of the issue, underlined by the neutron bomb experience, but also the growing
opposition to SALT in the United States and a number of
instances of transatlantic mis-communication in economic and
energy policy, presented the members of the NATO High-Level
Group, set up in mid-1978 to develop a policy, with an extremely
difficult task.

Official NATO doctrine offered no clear guidlines: a set of
Soviet systems ready to attack Western Europe seemed deserving
of a locally based response, but would not insistence on some
theatre nuclear balance confirm the separation of European-
based forces from those in the United States and also imply a
theatre conventional balance for which traditionally Europeans
had shown so little enthusiasm? What of the 'indivisibility of
deterrence' by which America's strategic arms were presumed
available as a response to any direct attack on any member of
NATO?

The formula the High Level Group decided upon reflected
NATO's complex political symbolism as much as the military
requirements which prompted the exercise in the first place. It
was to strengthen nuclear forces based in Europe but not by so
much that they would be seen to be equivalent in magnitude or
importance to those on the American continent. While it was
recognised that missiles carried on submarines were far safer from
surprise attack than those on land, ground-based systems were
preferred. For the military tasks planned, limited strikes against
specific targets to the enemy's rear, it was felt that submarine-
based missiles would lack close control, would be expensive and
not provide the physical presence required. A certain degree of
security from surprise attack could be found through mobility,
though unless the missiles were to wander constantly around the
European countryside, they would depend on warning time to be
removed from danger from pre-targeted Soviet missiles. The most

important advantage of a land-based system was the political value of being on European soil. By creating a risk of embroiling American nuclear missiles early on in an attack on Europe it reinforced the link between the United States and its allies while adding to deterrence against the Soviet Union.

Two missiles were available for introduction in the early 1980s – an extended-range version of the *Pershing* ballistic missiles already deployed in Germany and the new ground-launched cruise missile (GLCM). Neither of these was wholly satisfactory. Ballistic missiles were preferable to cruise missiles because they would not be troubled by air defences. The fact that the extended-range *Pershing* was a follow-on to an existing missile would make it politically less difficult than the GLCM which was already attracting controversy in SALT. However, *Pershing* lacked the range to cover all the required targets, save from West Germany. The decision was to have a mix of both systems.

The influence of Germany was largely felt in deciding upon the ownership and location of the new missiles. When nuclear weapons were first introduced into Europe in the late 1950s and early 1960s this was done by means of a 'double-key' system. This meant that European armies would control all but the actual warheads of the weapons. The warheads would be held by Americans who would arm the weapons if they were about to be used. The objective behind this clumsy device was mutual reassurance: neither would be able to drag the other into a nuclear war against its will. About half of the 7000 American warheads deployed in Europe are under this system of control, including many with British forces and also the first-generation *Pershing* missiles based in Germany, operated by German personnel. However, in the discussion of the modernisation programme the Germans argued for the weapons to be wholly controlled by the Americans under a single-key system. The longer range of the new weapons meant that strategic attacks could be launched against the Soviet territory for Germany, and it was felt to be less provocative if no German fingers were close to the relevant trigger. (The previous case of weapons of a range that could reach the Soviet Union – the 96 *Mace* B cruise missiles from 1962 to 1969 – were also on a single key.) Second, it was felt that the confidence in the commonality of NATO interests would be emphasised by not insisting on dual control. Apart from these political and

doctrinal questions, dual-key implies dual-ownership and therefore dual-finance. One of the more attractive features of the
proposed scheme was the American willingness to bear the
financial burden. A right to share the missile's control would
involve the right to share this burden.

The German role in the decision-making was largely negative
in that they insisted upon measures which would not throw their
own position into undue prominence. It was hoped to deflect
internal and external criticism of any increased connection between Germany and nuclear weapons by insisting that any new
programmes be endorsed by the alliance as a whole, and that it
was not to be alone in introducing the new weapons on to its
territory.

This latter condition, known as 'non-singularity', was not to be
satisfied by placing the weapons in Britain, for that was already
established as a nuclear power. Germany needed to share the
responsibility with another non-nuclear power. Greece and Turkey were too preoccupied with their own feud to be bothered.
Denmark and Norway had for many years refused to have any
nuclear weapons on their territory. Excluding the two small
countries Iceland and Luxembourg, that left Belgium, Holland
and Italy.

The 'non-singularity' condition was assumed to be dropping
the ball firmly in Holland's court. It was in Holland that the
anti-neutron bomb campaign had been most vociferous. Hostility
to the new weapon had been found in the Christian Democratic as
well as the Socialist Party, in religious as well as secular groups.
The high moral tone coming out of the country had irritated its
neighbours, especially Germany and Belgium who felt by impli-
cation that they were presumed to have less of an active con-
science. Because of its history, Germany felt vulnerable to accusa-
tions of militarism and therefore preferred to be seen acting in
concert with others.

By insisting on 'non-singularity', it appeared that the West
Germans were allowing NATO's plans to rest or fall on Dutch
participation, giving the smaller country extra power within the
alliance but also setting it a severe test of loyalty to NATO. This
led to intense speculation on the final Dutch position. However,
while Belgium's participation could be seen to be in some way
linked to that of Holland, Italy did not feel under any constraints.

Without any fuss the Italians decided to support the scheme, thus satisfying Germany's request and leaving Holland to sort out its own relations with NATO.

The final condition pushed by Germany but supported by most other Europeans was to decide upon an arms-control proposal in parallel with the weapons-modernisation programme. This was to placate the European arms-control constituency, but it could not have been easily avoided because of the extent to which the GLCM was already implicated in SALT. In the spring of 1979 a comparable group to the High-Level Group – this one known as the Special Group – began to consider TNF modernisation as a problem in arms control.

The basic outlines of the programme had been sorted out by the time the Nuclear Planning Group met in Florida in April 1979, when it was agreed that the details should be sorted out and the final decision taken by the end of the year. Past experience suggested that these issues benefited from a fixed timetable to concentrate official minds, avoid prevarication and allow little time for the opposition to mobilise. A December 1979 deadline also maintained some distance between the West German and American elections both scheduled for late 1980.

The effect of a firm deadline was also to make the issue something of a test of alliance cohesion. Increasingly the political need to take a difficult decision in unison came to be used as a potent argument in support of the programme irrespective of its actual merits.

By the time the High Level Group had completed its report in early autumn, reasonably strong consensus had been constructed in favour of proposals to deploy 108 *Pershing* II missiles and 464 GLCMs. Although deployment would start in 1983, the *Pershing* II force would not be completed until 1986 and the GLCM force until 1987.

Then came the expected attempt at disruption from the Soviet Union. On 6 October 1979 President Brezhnev made a major speech in East Berlin attempting to persuade NATO not to go ahead with the modernisation programme. He offered to reduce the number of Soviet missiles in Europe in arms control negotiations. As a unilateral gesture, 20,000 troops and 1000 tanks were to be moved out of East Germany, a retreat undertaken somewhat ostentatiously just before the NATO meeting in early December to consider the modernisation programme. If the modernisation was to go ahead, he warned, more Soviet missiles would soon be facing NATO and negotiations would become extremely difficult, if not impossible. In a more threatening tone he reminded those countries about to host new bases for long-range weapons that this would make them targets for attack.

This Soviet 'peace offensive' was rather clumsily constructed. There is an unwritten rule in arms control negotiations that serious new initiatives are made through diplomatic channels – to ensure that those for whom they are intended are properly prepared for the message – and not made with a blast of publicity, normally reserved for the scoring of propaganda points. By launching his proposals when he did, Brezhnev indicated that he was worried about the new NATO programme and this by itself offered an argument in NATO against abandoning the programme until substantial concessions were obtained from the Soviet Union. The concession that would have made a difference would have been a clear offer to reduce the number of SS-20s deployed. Once Soviet missile strength passed a certain point marginal addition or reductions would make little difference to NATO, certainly not enough to make it forgo a modern capability of its own. Finally, the Russians probably underestimated the extent to which NATO leaders had been chastened by the neutron bomb experience when it appeared that a Soviet propaganda campaign had succeeded in stopping a new military programme, and the extent to which this time the rationale for the programme was well understood and firmly supported.

To Soviet chagrin, the Brezhnev initiative was dismissed by NATO leaders in a somewhat brusque manner before it was felt prudent to offer a few words of encouragement, emphasising the readiness to engage in serious arms-control talks, but only after the theatre nuclear programme had been approved. There would always be an opportunity later to call it off, if there were good reason to do so. It seemed that NATO unity had held up well to the Soviet campaign, until doubts began to be heard in Scandinavia, Belgium and Holland, to the extent that in the latter two countries it was feared that the governments could fall if they pushed ahead with plans to base GLCMs on their soil. The Belgians, Dutch and Danes began to argue for delaying the deployment decision in order to give negotiations a chance.

BRITAIN

In Britain, there was none of the intensive discussion on the merits of theatre nuclear modernisation found in the rest of Europe – not even a Parliamentary debate. Within Government the key issue was whether Britain should participate more actively by purchasing a number of cruise missiles itself to replace the *Vulcan*.

The major interest of the Ministry of Defence in cruise missiles during 1978, was less to do with the problem of *Polaris* replacement than with *Vulcan* replacement. Fifty six of the old aircraft were still operational long after their sisters: the *Valiants* had succumbed to metal fatigue and the *Victors* had become tankers in the 1960s. Although still an impressive aircraft, the *Vulcan* was showing signs of age. Its operations and maintenance costs were growing and, with its large crew, was putting a strain on RAF manpower at a time when it was proving difficult to keep trained personnel. In 1969, when *Polaris* took over responsibility for the strategic deterrent, the *Vulcans* were kept prepared for long-range nuclear strikes and even given new 'lay down' bombs to replace the old *Blue Steel*, short-range missiles. The particular role was to attack the sort of targets normally assigned to TNFs in Europe – to the enemy rear relevant to the course of an ensuing land war, mainly the lines of communication bringing extra supplies of men, munitions and fuel to the front.

The cancellation of the TSR/2 and later the F-111 light bombers in the 1960s, because of their expense, had resulted in no new aircraft capable of fulfilling this role. The gap was partly to be filled by the new *Tornado* multi-role combat aircraft, which was billed (among other things) as a replacement for *Vulcan*. However, because this is a collaborative project, it does not have the deep strike capability which the other participating countries, particularly Germany, not only did not require but would have considered a positive embarrassment.

In 1977, the Ministry of Defence began to consider whether a new long-term weapon was needed to replace the *Vulcan*, now not expected to last much into the 1980s. This requirement was seen as quite separate from *Polaris* replacement. It was for the early 1980s – not the early 1990s.

The possibility of attempting to fit cruise missiles to the *Vulcans* themselves was considered, in an effort to prolong their active life in the same way that the United States was planning to prolong the active life of its B-52 heavy bombers with cruise missiles. Unfortunately the *Vulcans* were just too far past their prime to make this effort worthwhile. The problem with fitting cruise missiles to the new *Tornados* was that they were an awkward design for this purpose and could not carry a sufficient number. Far better would have been an adaptation of a wide-bodied jet, such as *Airbus*, but any new purpose-built system would be expensive.

At this point British decision-making was influenced by the NATO debate on TNFs. An option became open to Britain of purchasing some of the weapons to be prepared for NATO use for exclusive British use. The argument was that if there is to be a genuine European contribution to the NATO deterrent, it must have a flexibility on some rungs of the escalation ladder, and not just be able to come in at the final stage.

Of the two systems to be produced for NATO, *Pershing* could be ruled out because it could not hit Soviet targets if based in Britain. That left the GLCM, 160 of which were at any rate to be in Britain under the NATO scheme. If extra missiles were to be bought the country could replace *Vulcan* while benefiting once again from an American production line and logistics support.

A few senior policy-makers became extremely attracted to this idea, including the Chief of Defence Staff, Air Marshal Sir Neil Cameron, but in an active debate during 1979 and 1980 they failed to convince their colleagues. In doctrinal terms the 'decoupling' effects of European TNFs, making it possible for Europeans to destroy each other before the Americans felt at all implicated, were mentioned. However, the main objections were more practical. There was concern from the other service chiefs over making available more funds for new nuclear missions, at a time when plans were afoot for *Polaris* replacement and conventional capabilities also needed nourishment. There was some feeling that *Tornado* could perform some deep-strike role, even if not as deep as GLCM. The question was whether it was absolutely necessary for this role to be able to attack the USSR itself. That this represents a threshold for the Kremlin is clear from Soviet doctrine, but it might be one that, once passed, would signal the end of attempts at limited nuclear exchanges and a move to an all-out conflict, rather than a process of controlled escalation. The

other objection to presenting *Tornado* as a long-range TNF was
that it could embarrass the Germans, with *Tornados* of their own
and, eventually, cause problems in SALT in which they would be
difficult to accommodate.

The debate was more or less concluded by the very practical
problem of loading another new warhead programme on to
Aldermaston, when it was still recovering from the closure of some
of its capacity and the desertion of a number of key staff following
a scare over the leakage of radioactive materials in 1978. Not all
responsible were convinced that it could cope properly with a
Trident warhead, never mind an additional project.

Without a more direct involvement, the cost of the NATO
programme to Britain is remarkably cheap – a £10 million
contribution to infrastructure costs. The United States, which
would produce and own the missiles, will bear the brunt of the
estimated costs of £2.5 billion.

Outside Government the main concern was voiced by those
close to American bases in East Anglia and Oxfordshire where it
was assumed that the new missiles would be stationed. Given the
publicity surrounding the missiles the concern is not surprising
but whatever risks there might be are hardly novel. American
nuclear weapons have been based on British soil for some three
decades now. In 1977 the number of F-111s stationed in Britain
was increased with little protest. The difference is that the GLCM
sites will be more positively identified and that in a crisis they will
move off bases into the surrounding area. It is arguable that one of
the merits of the new programme is that it spreads the risk around
other NATO countries.

THE DECISION

In general Britain acted from the start and under Labour and
Conservative Governments, as an enthusiast for theatre nuclear
modernisation. Defence Secretary Francis Pym was active in
NATO arguing against any wavering. It was his line rather than
that of the Dutch, that was followed by NATO ministers on 12
December 1979 in their decision to go ahead. The Dutch and
Belgians did not reject the plans but wanted to observe the
development of arms control in Europe before finally agreeing to
accept the new weapons on their territory. The Dutch wanted 18

months to decide whether to opt in, and the Belgians 6 months to decide whether to opt out. It was felt politic not to include in the final communiqué mention of the numbers allocated to each country – 108 *Pershings* and 96 GLCMs to Germany; 160, 112, 48 and 48 GLCMs to Britain, Italy, Belgium and Holland respectively. (The British allocation was originally to be 124, but the Government agreed to take 36 extra when the Germans reported that it would be difficult for them to find space for 132 GLCMs).

Following the TNF decision little happened on the arms control front. NATO offered to negotiate on American TNFs in the context of SALT but then President Carter put SALT into the refrigerator (possibly the deep freeze) by asking the Senate to delay ratification. To the relief of many in NATO the Russians failed to exploit this contradictory position. Instead, they just rejected the NATO offer, refusing to negotiate unless the NATO programme was deferred and any discussions were broadened to include French and British systems. Both the smaller nuclear powers had made it clear that they would not permit this. Lacking flexibility in their force structures, they would have no bargaining position in the negotiations. Instead of using its nuclear force to gain access to the 'top table', Britain preferred to stay away from the 'top table' to protect its nuclear force.

12 Rationales

The main aim of this book thus far has been to describe, as fully as possible, the evolution of British nuclear weapons policy and the factors that have influenced it. However, it would be wrong to conclude without some attempt to assess the arguments for and against Britain remaining a nuclear power.

What is impressive about official statements on the role of the nuclear force, apart from their rarity and brevity, is not the adaptation to the shifts in the international context but their unchanging character. The description decided upon in the 1950s – 'a contribution to NATO's nuclear deterrent' – remains. In fact, the force is normally described as 'the independent nuclear deterrent', as if its independence and deterrent effect are beyond dispute. Moreover, the nature of the deterrent effect it is supposed to produce reflects a formula hit upon in the early 1960s and found convenient ever since.

A SECOND CENTRE OF DECISION

We noted earlier that Denis Healey, when Defence Secretary in the 1960s, picked up the notion of independent nuclear decision-centres as an impressive rationale for the British force in the 1960s, as it allowed both for loyalty to NATO and the playing of an independent role. It had already, in essence, been adopted by officials of the Ministry of Defence and they have found it useful ever since on any occasion when they, or their ministers, have been called upon to justify the deterrent. A 1974 Memorandum from the Ministry, for example, explained how a *Polaris* force:

gives NATO a separate centre of decision-making in Europe which the Soviets must take into account (the French strategic deterrent is not committed to the alliance); it increases the credibility of the overall NATO deterrent; and it provides an element of insurance, and reassurance to our European allies, against any weakening of the United States nuclear guarantee.[1]

In 1979 first a Labour and then a Conservative Secretary of State for Defence used similar reasoning to explain the value of the deterrent. In January, Fred Mulley told a Parliamentary Committee:

[The deterrent] provides a second centre of nuclear decision-making within the Alliance. This would complicate the calculations of a possible aggressor when contemplating aggression, although we have no ways of calculating the extent of this effect. Our allies welcome a situation in which the United States is not expected to bear the whole burden of nuclear decision-making.[2]

In October, his successor, Francis Pym, in a speech to his party conference said:

Our own deterrent will enable the United States, whose contribution is, of course, . . . crucial . . . to share the burden of nuclear decision-making which it would otherwise have to bear entirely alone. It will powerfully increase the uncertainty in Soviet planning.[3]

At the start of 1980 Mr Pym provided the most complete statement of this theory of twin decision-centres to the House of Commons. It is worth quoting at length:

Our strategy seeks to influence Soviet calculations fundamentally and decisively. It seeks to guard against any risk of Soviet miscalculation. The United States, by their words and deeds, has constantly made clear its total commitment to come to the aid of Europe, and to help to defend Europe by whatever means are necessary, without exception. No words or deeds in advance could make that more crystal clear. But we are of course dealing with possible situations that would be without precedent in history, and of unique peril.

The decision to take nuclear action, at any time, would be vastly hard for any President of the United States to take. In recent years I think that it has become even harder, if that is imaginable, because of the fact of super-power nuclear parity. The British Government have the greatest confidence in the weight and reality of the United States commitment. We cast no shade of doubt upon it. What matters most is not what we think but what the Russians think. . . .

The Russians cannot be assumed to look at the world as we do. . . . In a crisis, Soviet leaders – perhaps beset by some pressures of turmoil in the Soviet empire, perhaps looking out upon a NATO Alliance passing through some temporary phase of internal difficulty – might conceivably misread American resolution. They might be tempted to gamble on United States hesitation.

The nuclear decision, whether as a matter of retaliatory response or in another circumstance, would, of course, be no less agonising for the United Kingdom than for the United States. But it would be a decision of a separate and independent Power, and a Power whose survival in freedom might be more directly and closely threatened by aggression in Europe than that of the United States. This is where the fact of having to face two decision-makers instead of one is of such significance.

Soviet leaders would have to assess that there was a greater chance of one of them using its nuclear capability than if there were a single decision-maker across the Atlantic. The risk to the Soviet Union would be inescapably higher and less calculable. This is just another way of saying that the deterrence of the Alliance as a whole would be the stronger, the more credible and therefore the more effective.[4]

The attraction of this approach lies as much in its diplomatic convenience as in the rigour of its strategic logic. It allows Britain to maintain an independent force, while insisting that this is mainly for the greater good of the alliance. It picks up a compelling argument in favour of an independent capability – inevitable doubts about the credibility of the US nuclear guarantee – but desists from endorsing it, warning only that the Russians may accept these doubts. It does not pretend that deterrence works on a certainty of nuclear retaliation, only that there can be no

certainty that retaliation will be withheld. There is a simple
syllogism: uncertainty improves deterrence; the outcomes of two
sets of decisions are more uncertain than one; therefore a condition involving two sets of decisions improves deterrence.

This argument has some merit but it is not without flaws. One
problem lies in assuming that it is uncertainty *per se* that is
valuable for deterrence. Some forms of certainty, for example
encouraging confidence that all members of the alliance would act
in an emergency as they claim they will act, contribute to deterrence. It is only when the clarification of the alliance position
would reveal hesitation and inhibition that a certain amount of
ambiguity and enigma has value.

One way in which the stress on separate decisions may detract
from deterrence is by casting doubt on the quality of the decision-
making procedures of the alliance as a whole. Final decisions on
British nuclear use 'rest solely with the British Prime Minister'.
This independence is no more than any sovereign state would
expect. At the same time, the commitment of Britain's nuclear
forces to NATO, the fact that they are targeted together with
those of the United States, and the importance of the alliance's
consultative mechanisms are also stressed, raising the question of
whether, if mechanisms work as they should, there will be significant divergence between British and American policy. Furthermore, an important advantage of Britain's force is supposed to be
the influence it provides over American policy and decisions.

If, as is quite conceivable, it is the question of using tactical
nuclear weapons based in Germany that comes up first, then the
consultations become even more complicated. The NATO
guidelines on this matter, agreed in Athens in 1962, provide for
'special weight' to be 'accorded the views of these NATO countries on or from whose territories nuclear weapons would be
employed, countries providing the nuclear warheads, or the
countries providing or manning nuclear delivery systems'. The
guidelines recognise the 'necessity of avoiding inflexible or overly
elaborate procedures which might inhibit action or endanger the
credibility of the deterrent'.[5] The tension between efficient, agreed
action and safeguards to national sovereignty appears most
keenly at this level. If any fighting could not be stopped by
conventional means, the manner in which the question of tactical
nuclear use was resolved would shape later discussion on strategic
nuclear use.

The credibility of tactical nuclear weapons suffers from the presumption that any divergence of views would hold up the most urgent request for a decision. In this multiple-decision centres represent an unavoidable problem for NATO rather than an asset. If official NATO consultative mechanisms are to be effective, then emphasising the possibility of surprises from the British may not be helpful to the alliance.

If any increment of deterrence is to accrue from extra decision-centres, rather than a source of delay and confusion in forming a wartime policy, then it must lie in the possibility that a British Prime Minister, surrounded by faint hearts unwilling to take the plunge, would initiate nuclear hostilities. Much publicity has been given to the possible 'catalytic', 'detonator' or 'trigger' effect of early nuclear use by a small power on the subsequent behaviour of the super-powers. A small nuclear power could undermine the efforts of the super-powers to keep a military crisis under control at the expense of European interest, by introducing nuclear weapons and accelerating the process of escalation. The argument relies on the irrationality of the situation which might make such a move plausible. In this it is not dissimilar from other NATO theories which rely on the deterrent threat of matters getting out of control.

It is nonetheless difficult to explain the interests which would prompt such recklessness by a small power, or the mechanisms which would produce the intended effect of drawing the United States nuclear arsenal into the conflict (rather than simply the full weight of Soviet might being visited upon the offending power while the United States stood by, horrified but passive). In the scenario which dominates NATO planning, involving a Warsaw Pact attack on Germany, British interests would not be in hurrying along the process of escalation. Current British policy supports NATO's doctrine of forward defence, in part because it is desirable that any fighting should be kept as far away as possible from the British Isles. The more intense the war the more Britain would suffer. While not inconceivable, it remains unlikely that a British Prime Minister would wish to introduce nuclear weapons before it was absolutely unavoidable. Certainly comments by British politicians when speaking unofficially do not encourage the view that a British finger is most likely to be the first to press the nuclear button.

For example, before becoming Minister for the Royal Air Force in the current Government, Geoffrey Pattie MP, wrote that:

> The only really credible scenario is the threatened use of the
> strategic system in order to deter a nuclear attack on the United
> Kingdom itself. . . . British public opinion is most unlikely to
> approve the use of strategic weapons in response to a direct
> conventional attack on British interests and forces, no matter
> where such an attack takes place.[6]

Not surprisingly, American Administrations have never been
particularly enamoured with the 'trigger' theory, and have insisted that any decisions on the use of their nuclear forces would
be deliberate and considered. It has not been felt a sensible idea
for Britain to promote, so long as it is anxious to demonstrate that
it is a worthy and responsible recipient of American hardware.

The difficulty in imagining scenarios in which there might be
any cause for Britain to use nuclear weapons independently was
stressed in a debate in the House of Lords by Lord Carver, a
former Chief of Defence Staff. He noted that he had been concerned with the subject for 21 years:

> Over the years the arguments have shifted and I have heard
> them all; but in that time I have never heard or read a scenario
> which I would consider to be realistic in which it could be
> considered to be right or reasonable for the Prime Minister or
> Government of this country to order the firing of our indepen-
> dent strategic force at a time when the Americans were not
> prepared to fire theirs – certainly not before Russian nuclear
> weapons had landed in this country. And, again, if they had
> already landed, would it be right and reasonable? All it would
> do would be to invite further retaliation.[7]

As samples of attempts at imaginative scenarios we can note
two books providing speculative accounts of the course of World
War Three published in 1978. Both have Britain involved in the
opening shots of the nuclear exchange (more one presumes to
engage the interest of British readers than through strategic
analysis). In General Sir John Hackett, *The Third World War*[8] the
Soviet Union destroys Birmingham in a nuclear strike in order to
impress a summit conference of Western leaders, meeting in
London after a Soviet conventional offensive had ground to a halt,

with the danger of not acceding to Soviet demands. The choice of a British city depends wholly on the presence of Western leaders in London. In Hackett's account the existence of an independent British nuclear force does not appear in Soviet calculations. In Brigadier Shelford Bidwell (ed) *World War 3*,[9] hard-pressed British forces in Germany use tactical nuclear weapons, though it is unclear from the account who takes the decision, for prior to hostilities the British had decided not to use nuclear weapons. This first use is followed by American nuclear attacks on military targets in the combat zone. The Soviet response is to attack US Air Force bases in East Anglia with the intention of putting the British in a capitulationist mood, to remove the only American air bases inaccessible to Soviet ground troops, and to demonstrate Soviet resolution to the US President, but not to initiate all-out nuclear exchange (in this they fail). Again, no mention is made of British *Polaris* missiles influencing Soviet calculations.

All this may merely indicate the limits to imagination (and the reluctance of British Army officers to think in nuclear terms). It can be argued that any scenarios involving nuclear use by anybody defy comprehension because any use of nuclear weapons would be irrational, but that we are talking about exceptional international circumstances which are not conducive to rationality. Furthermore the whole theory of separate decision-makers rests on its influence on Soviet calculations. What matters are Soviet perceptions, on which our knowledge is, to say the least, imperfect.

Soviet references to the British and French forces acknowledge their destructive power but attempt to refute the theory of proportionality. This theory holds that the smaller prize offered by the smaller powers (and Britain perhaps is becoming a smaller prize all the time) means that they do not have to threaten the same amount of retaliation as a super-power. The USSR observes that in a nuclear exchange between Britain and itself, the devastation of Russia would be less than complete while that of Britain would be total. The Soviet comment on Mr Pym's speech on British nuclear weapons policy was that 'people in glass houses shouldn't throw stones'.

This makes it difficult to disprove the contention that a separate centre of nuclear decision is of benefit to NATO, but it does indicate that its foundations may be weak. There is also the question as to whether expenditure on a successor to *Polaris* may be the best allocation of British resources on behalf of NATO in the 1980s and 1990s.

CONTRIBUTIONS TO NATO

In 1974 the alliance formally endorsed the British and French nuclear forces, in tones that were somewhat less than ringing, when it was noted that they were 'capable of playing a deterrent role of their own'.[10] It has been assumed that the non-nuclear allies have seen British and French forces as something of an extravagance and that scarce funds could be more usefully spent on conventional forces. There is evidence that views on this in recent years may have changed, particularly in Germany, for reasons mentioned in the previous two chapters. Nevertheless while Britain's allies may be pleased that it purchases all manner of military capabilities, they have not necessarily faced up to its resource predicament. When and if the budgetary crunch, described in Chapter 8, appears, they may not be pleased if the nuclear force survives only through reduced contributions to conventional forces. There is a danger that the cost of maintaining nuclear forces in Europe and America may push NATO, inadvertently, towards excessive dependence on nuclear threats with only a slight capacity for conventional defence.

Against this, supporters of the nuclear force argue that it is mistaken to assume that funds saved by abandoning the force would be spent on conventional forces rather than just lost to the defence budget. It is suggested that the nuclear force raises the whole tone of the British defence effort which would generally begin to go downhill without it. (For some, of course, this would make the end of a nuclear role an even more attractive option.) Nevertheless, noting these observations it is hard to avoid the conclusion that major expenditure on a successor to *Polaris* will pose a major question of defence priorities, if only because of the weaknesses in the British economy.

A second problem in presenting the nuclear force as a contribution to NATO is that there is a respectable case for arguing that it makes it easier to opt out of a war involving the rest of the alliance, similar to a case often employed in France. In, for example, a situation where the Russians are attempting to undermine the cohesion of NATO by picking on individual allies, the ability of

Britain to respond in kind might divert Soviet attention elsewhere. The advantage of being an island creates a sanctuary
against conventional attack, albeit incomplete. A 'sanctuary'
strategy is, if anything, more plausible for Britain than France,
which would find it extremely difficult to keep out of any fighting
in neighbouring territory. However, the links with the United
States may be too great for Britain to get away with this approach.
There are too many US nuclear bases in the British Isles for the
Soviet Union to ignore in even a limited nuclear war.

The only version of this theory that does not hint at disloyalty to
NATO is the argument that, in current alliance strategy, the
British Isles play an essential role as a staging post for reserves
coming over from the United States. The knowledge of possible
retaliation for any nuclear attack on Britain would undermine
Soviet temptations to destroy this forward base for the Americans
before it can be put to use, or to attack the reserves when they
arrive before they embark for the continent. This may at least
make it more tolerable for Britain to act as an American base but
it does not remove nuclear threats to the reserves, which could still
be caught as they disembark on the continent. The benefit is in
staving off the initiation of nuclear war by the Soviet Union by a
limited attack on military targets in Britain. It provides little help
on the decisions that might have to be taken if NATO is contemplating first use of nuclear weapons, or if nuclear exchanges have
already begun in and around the European battlefield.

Nevertheless a decision to opt out of the nuclear battle seems as
likely as one to opt in, and is hinted at in the theory of separate
decision-centres, with the motivation one of unheroic hesitancy
and caution rather than unnatural valour.

INSURANCE POLICY

The fact that the preferred doctrine accompanying Britain's
nuclear capability is not wholly convincing, does not mean that
strategic rationales for the nuclear forces are exhausted or wholly
specious: only that their articulation can be diplomatically awkward. This is largely because they involve questioning the word
and good faith of the United States, which is the benefactor of
Britain in upholding its nuclear status and whose protection is
still at the centre of security policy.

When Mr Pym outlined the official doctrine in his speech to
Parliament he first dismissed, rather brusquely, alternative forms
of justification:

> political prestige, our status in the Alliance or a comparison
> with France. One hears sometimes an argument made out for
> the concept of a 'Fortress Britain' – some kind of insurance
> policy concept, should the United States go isolationist or the
> Alliance collapse.[11]

We will discuss political rationales presently. For the moment
we can note that debates over the American commitment constitute an important undercurrent in the British debate. Officials
note that we may be grateful for our own nuclear forces if and
when the alliance ceases to exist, but refrain from hypotheses on
the circumstances that might cause its demise. On occasion they
become more explicit, as the Ministry of Defence did in evidence
to the Expenditure Committee in 1975, when it noted the value of
the British force as 'an element of insurance, and reassurance to
our European allies, against any weakening of the United States
nuclear guarantee'. It then went on to claim that:

> In the last resort, if the Alliance was to collapse, the possession
> of an independent strategic weapon provides the United King-
> dom with the means of preserving national security by deter-
> ring large scale conventional or nuclear attack or of countering
> nuclear blackmail.[12]

In less official pronouncements the theme of the inadequacy of
the US nuclear guarantee comes increasingly to the fore. Consider
the following sample from memoranda submitted by Conservative MPs to the Expenditure Committee. Neville Trotter MP:

> With the Soviets now in a position of equality . . . it seems much
> less certain that US President would be prepared to commit his
> country to the horrors of major nuclear attack if Britain rather
> than America was the subject of an initial nuclear assault. We
> must therefore continue to possess our own capability for
> nuclear retaliation.

Geoffrey Pattie MP after suggesting that the strategic advantage
in the 1980s will lie with the Soviet Union:

It is no more than a blinding glimpse of the obvious to say that a guarantee which is no longer automatic is no longer a guarantee and despite the presence of US forces on the ground in Europe in no way can there now be said to be an American nuclear guarantee protecting Western Europe'.[13]

The idea of Britain acting independently is often derided on the grounds that it relies so much on the United States. This derision is usually excessive. The United States could not physically prevent Britain launching its nuclear weapons if it wanted to do so. While British weapons are assigned to their targets by a multinational group at the headquarters of the US Strategic Air Command at Omaha there is no reason in principle why another set of targets could not be substituted if necessary. The only real question mark relates to communication between the authorities ashore and the submarine. The only means of communicating with a submerged submarine is Very Low Frequency (VLF) radio. The major British VLF station is Rugby. The station at Simonstown in South Africa is no longer available. Whether this also applies to the station at Halifax in Canada is not known. It would be very surprising if the authorities relied solely on Rugby as this would be an obvious target in any pre-emptive attack. It is therefore likely that some alternative means of communication are available, and some of these may go through the Americans.

The real consequences of any American withdrawal of support from the British force would only be felt over time. Britain would be unable to test its missiles or warheads to ensure continued reliability. There would be a loss of supplies of nuclear materials and spare parts for those elements of the force purchased from America. Intelligence on Soviet targets would become out of date, as information from reconnaissance satellites was no longer passed on.

All this would cause serious but not insuperable problems which, at some cost, could probably be solved by developing production of key components at home. The major difficulties would come with testing facilities and intelligence, but unless the break with the United States came in the middle of a new programme the consequences should not be too serious.

The extent of any disruption would depend on the nature of the divorce of Britain and the United States. If the United States became nervous in a European crisis and decided to stay out of things, Britain could act alone. As it would take time for the loss of American support to impair Britain's capacity for independent action, the real danger is of a fundamental shift in United States policy to Europe. It is not inconceivable that the United States might renounce its obligations to Europe in a state of high dudgeon, severing abruptly a military relationship built up over decades, but a withdrawal is as likely to be undertaken in such a way as to help strengthen Europe's own forces by way of compensation. A book recently published in the United States advocates, quite seriously as a second-best policy, American disengagement from Europe combined with aid in strengthening a united European deterrent (partly on the grounds that Europe will not unite while it depends on the United States).[14] If the divorce was more in sorrow than in anger, then the British force should be able to survive without serious disability.

The real difficulty comes in imagining the circumstances in which Britain would want to act independently. The nuclear force might be said to have three possible roles. First, in a cruel world of increasing disorder Britain could revert to a splendid isolation, protecting itself from predators by threats of retaliation while avoiding active engagement in international politics. Second, in the shock following the collapse of NATO, there may be an attempt to organise a European Defence Community, with the same function as NATO. Britain, with France, might then be asked to pool its nuclear resources to construct a European deterrent. Third, Britain, perhaps again with France, might attempt to play the role of nuclear guarantor for its partners currently played by the United States.

This last option is the most unlikely. The pressures that undermine the credibility of the American guarantee will be doubly effective with Britain and France. If the Americans had failed in their duty there would be no reason to trust much smaller powers to take their place. The only credible small European deterrent would be German, because West Germany has the common border with the Warsaw Pact and could threaten a nuclear riposte to invasion with more certainty than others who might tolerate the loss of some German territory before committing themselves on nuclear use. However, for the moment, the prospect of German nuclear capability alarms its neighbours and the idea is generally discouraged, in Bonn as much as anywhere else.

The European deterrent of a united community might be a more promising line, but this requires political developments that are for the moment quite distant. It is not inconceivable that pressure of circumstances will force the Europeans together into a common defence community. This was once thought to be a natural progression in international affairs, but the experience of the 1970s does not offer encouragement to proponents of an integrated Europe.

We return to the point that a replacement for *Polaris* will be operating in the next century. It is virtually impossible to offer convincing scenarios on how and when a nuclear capability might be of value, but it is equally difficult to assert with confidence that there never would be circumstances when the British would be grateful for a last-resort deterrent. The responsibility for removing forever that capability would be a difficult one for any British government to accept.

The most compelling strategic rationale for a British nuclear force, therefore, resides less in the immediate requirements of British defence than in the uncertainties of the future. It is a rationale that has an appeal that is more primitive than intellectual, but is no less powerful for that.

The most compelling strategic argument against a nuclear force lies in consideration of the proper allocation of scare defence resources. A declining contribution to conventional forces increases reliance on nuclear weapons, making any East–West conflict more dangerous, and is also likely to cause controversy with Britain's allies as they are asked to take up discarded responsibilities.

POLITICAL RATIONALES

It has often been believed in the past that a nuclear arsenal ensures that a country has a prominent position in international politics. Whether or not nuclear weapons may be necessary for great power status, they are certainly not sufficient. Britain has managed to combine its nuclear status with a general decline in its international position. In the various crises and conflicts of the past years, a British nuclear force has been barely relevant, except perhaps, in a negative sense, in early attempts to join the Common Market.

For the moment it brings no diplomatic advantage, except for an ability to speak with some authority whenever nuclear matters are discussed, such as NATO's Nuclear Planning Group or arms-control negotiations. However, with no surplus capacity in its nuclear programmes to bargain away in negotiations, Britain is attempting to stay out of SALT rather than participate.

The political harm that comes from the nuclear programme may be as slight as the political good. It is not an object of international controversy, and it cannot be said to be responsible for recent stages in the arms race or nuclear proliferation. Those who argue that to abandon the force would, in its exemplary wisdom, galvanise the enlightened opinion of mankind into steps to rid the world of these awful weapons exaggerate the extent to which countries would allow this to influence their own strategic calculations. It would be seen more as a symptom of Britain's decline than an impressive gesture.

The political case for abandoning a nuclear role, in fact, lies mainly in coming to terms with the country's decline. In one of the more forceful contributions to the Commons debate on nuclear weapons, Labour MP Robin Cook commented:

It is time that we adjusted ourselves to the fact that we are a declining medium-range power and looked first and foremost at how we use our desperately scarce industrial resources to commercial advantage rather than on grandiose projects which we have inherited from the past.[15]

The problem perhaps lies in admitting defeat in an attempt to keep up with the world's major nations. The centres of European power are now in Paris and Bonn. It is admitted within Whitehall that it would rankle, again for emotional as much as intellectual reasons, to leave France as the only European nuclear power, confirming its ascendancy over Britain. To have a nuclear arsenal still demands some sort of respect and, in circumstances difficult to predict, it might be the most valuable source of international power.

CONCLUSION

The politics of beginning or terminating some activity are usually far more difficult and complicated than the politics of carrying on as before. To add or subtract a nuclear capability would command attention: to maintain it would barely be noticed. This is why it seems likely that Britain will continue to be a nuclear power well into the next century. It would appear from an opinion poll published in November 1979 that this would have the overwhelming support of the electorate. The poll showed 82 per cent in favour of an independent nuclear deterrent, 13 per cent in favour of depending only on the alliance and only 5 per cent in favour of having nothing to do with nuclear weapons. It is of note that 40 per cent believed a major war quite likely by the end of the century and two-thirds felt that if it did come it would most probably involve the use of nuclear weapons against Britain, which indicates both a pessimism as to the future and an implicit doubt as to the efficacy of the British nuclear deterrent.[16]

The discussion in this chapter only hints at a broader strategic debate on national and alliance policies. The argument presented has not been in favour of, or against, the British nuclear force; only to suggest that the choice is difficult and in some ways marginal, given the state of our understanding of international strategy and politics. The nuclear force's current political role is not particularly constructive or destructive. It neither contributes much nor detracts from NATO strategy. It neither supports nor precludes a more neutralist foreign policy. It is not abnormally expensive for a major military capability but future money will have to be found at a time when the economy is weak and the overall defence budget will be under pressure. The argument against rests on an assessment of immediate priorities. The argument in favour rests on a fear of an unknown and dangerous future, and an assumption that an adversary would think longer and harder before taking on another nuclear power than it would before taking on a country with a solely conventional capacity for resistance.

The world is likely to contain vast nuclear arsenals of enormous destructive power for the indefinite future. It is because of this that the future is so indefinite. Some four decades ago, at the very start of the nuclear era, Britain played a crucial part in being the first to demonstrate that an atomic bomb was both a theoretical and a practical proposition. Many subsequent decisions, mainly taken in Washington and Moscow, have ensured that the overbearing role of nuclear weapons in contemporary international affairs is now so well established as to be virtually beyond political choice. Whether the world is to have nuclear powers is no longer an issue for British policy: the question is how to exist in such a world.

Appendix 1   Submarines

	Date laid down	Date launched	Date commissioned	Date of first patrol
HMS *Resolution**	26.2.64	15.9.66	2.10.67	6.68
HMS *Renown*†	25.6.64	25.2.67	15.11.68	8.69
HMS *Repulse**	12.3.65	4.11.67	28.9.68	6.6/
HMS *Revenge*†	19.5.65	15.3.68	4.12.69	9.70

* Built at Vickers, Barrow-in-Furness.
† Built at Cammell Laird, Birkenhead.

A *Polaris* boat has a surface displacement of 7500 tons, a sub-merged displacement of some 8500 tons, is 425 feet long, has an estimated minimum submerged speed of about 30 knots and carries a complement of 14 officers and 129 ratings (divided more or less equally between engine room, missiles and general systems). It is fitted with six 21-inch torpedo tubes in addition to lauch tubes for ballistic missiles. The boats are powered by one British NR2 pressurised water turbine coupled to a single screw. The primary navigation system is an inertial set (Ship's Inertial Navigation System – SINS) which constantly calculates the present position by dead reckoning, using an array of accelerometers. Several communications systems are fitted, the most important of which is very low frequency (VLF) radio. Sonar equipment for the detection of and location of other submarines is also fitted.

SOURCE: Ian Smart, *The Future of the British Nuclear Deterrent, Technical Economic and Strategic Issues* (London: RIIA, 1977) as well as personal sources.

Appendix 2 Characteristics of SLBMs

	Polaris A-3	*Poseidon C-3*	*Trident C-4*
Initial operational capability (US)	1964	1971	1979
Initial operational capability (UK)	1967	—	1992(?)
Stages	2	2	3
Fuel	Solid	Solid	Solid
Length (feet)	31.3	34.1	34.1
Diameter (feet)	4.5	6.2	6.2
Range (nautical miles)	2500	2500	4000
Guidance	Inertial	Inertial	Inertial: digital computer
Weight (pounds)	35,000	64,000	70,000 (approx)
Throw-weight (pounds)	1000	2000–3000	3000+
Warheads×Yield (US) (kilotons)	3×200 (MRV)	10×50 (MIRV)	8×100 (MIRV)
Warheads×Yield (UK) (kilotons)	3×200 (MRV)*	—	?

* A new warhead has been developed for the UK Polaris. Its precise configuration is not known.

SOURCE: A. A. Tinajero, *Protected Strategic Offensive Weapons Inventories of the US and USSR* (Washington DC, Congressional Research Service, 1977); Colin Gray, *The Future of Land-Based Missile Forces* Adelphi Paper 140 (London: IISS, 1977).

Appendix 3 Expenditure on Nuclear Weapons

	Nuclear strategic forces		Special materials†	'Other R&D‡	Total defence
	V-bombers*	Polaris			
1963–4					1870
1964–5	186	186			2000
1965–6			42		2120
1966–7	45	60	55	33	2172
1967–8	39	65	40	32	2205
1968–9	25	70	31	27	2271
1969–70	5	55	32	23	2266
1970–1		32	24	17	2280
1971–2		34	20	19	2545
1972–3		38		37	2854
1973–4		39		51	3365
1974–5		48		78	3800
1975–6		58		109	4548
1976–7		78		139	5632
1977–8		96		158	6329
1978–9		93		161	6919
1979–80		126		184	8558

Note: figures are in current £million.

* From 1970 to 1971 the V-bombers come under the line item strike/recce under Air General Purpose Forces.

† 'Special materials' included materials for nuclear warheads and bombs and for the propulsion units of all nuclear submarines. This line item did not appear separately after 1971–2. This is now incorporated into the figure for strategic nuclear forces, of which it constitutes a small proportion.

‡ R&D on the strategic nuclear forces is covered under the heading 'other R&D'. This also includes expenditure on the management of the whole R&D effort in MOD, work undertaken using MOD facilities and personnel for other Government departments, and also work on tactical nuclear weapons.

SOURCES: *Annual Defence Estimates; Twelfth Report from the Expenditure Committee,* Session 1972/3; MOD.

Appendix 4   Breakdown of Costs of Nuclear Strategic Forces (excluding R&D)

	1966–7	1967–8	1968–9	1969–70	1970–1	1971–2	1972–3	1973–4	1974–5	1975–6	1976–7	1977–8	1978–9	1979–80
Capital production	45.3	47.9	45.3	30.4	8.6	0.7	6.3	6.5	7.2	10.5	16.5	15.4	17.2	28.4
Capital costs	5.9	4.1	2.1	2.7	0.7	0.7	1.0	1.4	3.2	4.3	5.9	8.0	3.2	4.1
Personnel	2.2	3.6	7.5	9.5	10.2	12.5	11.8	12.4	13.2	19.2	25.1	29.1	29.0	36.7
Other running costs	6.3	9.6	15.1	12.6	12.1	13.7	18.9	18.7	24.4	24.0	30.5	43.8	43.6	57.2
TOTAL	59.7	65.2	70.0	55.2	31.6	33.8	38.0	39.0	48.0	58.0	78.0	96.3	93.0	126.4

Note: figures are in current £million

* The figures in the table are based on the functional analysis of Estimates for each year and reflect the prices ruling at the time. Since Estimates for 1979–80 were presented at forecast outturn price levels, there is, in effect, a gap of 2 years' inflation between the figures for 1978–9 and 1979–80. No account is taken of Supplementary Estimates.

SOURCE: *Second Report from the Expenditure Committee,* Session 1971–2, p. 334; MOD.

Appendix 5 Manpower

	Civilian personnel		Military personnel	
	Nuclear strategic Forces	Other R&D	Nuclear strategic Forces	Other R&D
1969–70	2,800	3,600	4,200	N/A
1970–1	3,300	4,000	3,200	N/A
1971–2	3,800	2,500	3,000	N/A
1972–3	3,600	2,500	2,200	N/A
1973–4	3,500	10,800	2,200	100
1974–5	3,200	15,100	2,100	600
1975–6	3,800	15,200	2,600	500
1976–7	4,100	13,400	2,800	400
1977–8	4,200	12,900	2,800	400
1978–9	4,100	12,100	2,800	400
1979–80	4,400	11,600	2,500	400

Notes:

Other R&D involves the management of the overall R&D programme and work undertaken for other Government Departments.

In 1973–4, other R&D came to include staff of UK Atomic Energy Authority that was being transferred to the Ministry of Defence. These personnel work on propulsion units for nuclear submarines and 'tactical' nuclear weapons, as well as 'strategic' nuclear weapons.

N/A indicates not available.

Appendix 6 *Polaris* Missile Tests

1. There have been 22 test firing of UK *Polaris* missiles to date. This number comprises 14 DASO (Demonstration and Shakedown Operation) firings from submerged submarines off the Florida coast following commissioning and subsequent re-fits of each boat, and are part of the testing of readiness of submarine, *Polaris* weapon sub-systems and crews to enter the operational cycle. The dates of these firings were:

HMS *Resolution* 15 Feb and 4 Mar 1968; 6 Mar 1972; 14 July 1977.
HMS *Repulse* 27 Mar and 14 Apr 1969; 13 Feb 1973; 20 Feb 1979.
HMS *Renown* 24 July and 11 Aug 1969; 16 July 1974.
HMS *Revenge* 1 and 18 June 1970; 22 Nov 1975.

2. The remaining eight firings were from the ground at Cape Canaveral and took place on:

12 Sept 1977	4 Apr 1979
8 Nov 1977	5 July 1979
27 July 1978	31 Aug 1979
30 Nov 1978	8 Nov 1979

SOURCE: MOD.

Appendix 7   Underground Nuclear Tests

Nine underground nuclear tests have been carried out on behalf of the UK at the US Department of Energy's test site at Nevada. The tests have been conducted under the Agreement for Co-operation on the Uses of Atomic Energy for Mutual Defence Purposes, which has been in effect between the two countries since 4 August 1958. The names, dates and yields of tests are:

Name	Date	Yield
Pampas	1 Mar 1962	Low (less than 20 kilotons)
Tendrac	7 Dec 1962	Low (less than 20 kilotons)
Cormorant	17 July 1964	Low (less than 20 kilotons)
Charcoal	10 Sept 1965 ⎱	Within the range of 20–200
Fallon	23 May 1974 ⎰	kilotons
Banon	26 Aug 1976 ⎫	
Fondutta	11 Apr 1978 ⎪	All within the range of 20–150
Quargel	18 Nov 1978 ⎬	kilotons
Nessel	29 Aug 1979 ⎭	

SOURCE: MOD.

Notes

NOTES TO CHAPTER 1

1. The story of Britain's involvement in atomic energy up to 1952 has been well told by the official historian of the United Kingdom Atomic Energy Authority, Margaret Gowing, *Britain and Atomic Energy, 1939–1945* (London: Macmillan, 1964) and the two volumes entitled *Independence and Deterrence* (London: Macmillan, 1974).
2. *Defence: Outline of Future Policy: 1957*, Cmnd 124.
3. *Report on Defence: Britain's Contribution to Peace and Security: 1958*, Cmnd 363, p. 2.
4. *Hansard*, vol. 537, col. 2182 (2 March 1955). British policy-making and debates on this matter are admirably described in Andrew Pierre, *Nuclear Politics: The British Experience with an Independent Strategic Force, 1939–1970* (London: Oxford University Press, 1970). See also John Groom, *British Thinking about Nuclear Weapons* (London: Frances Pinter, 1974).
5. A full account of all aspects of this collaboration is found in a memorandum by Dr John Simpson on 'The Anglo-American Nuclear Relationship and its Implications for the Choice of a Possible Successor to the Current Polaris Force', *The Future of the United Kingdom's Nuclear Weapons Policy*, Sixth Report from the Expenditure Committee, Session 1978–9.

NOTE TO CHAPTER 2

1. So remarkable in fact that President Kennedy asked Professor Richard Neustadt to prepare a study of the matter. A version appears in Professor Neustadt's *Alliance Politics* (New York: Columbia University Press, 1970).

NOTES TO CHAPTER 3

1. *Statement on Defence: 1964*, Cmnd 2270, p. 6.
2. Harold Wilson, *The Labour Government 1964–1970* (London: Weidenfeld & Nicolson and Michael Joseph, 1979), pp. 42, 55.

3. Pierre, op. cit., p. 278.
4. Bruce Reed and Geoffrey Williams, *Denis Healey and the Policies of Power* (London: Sidgwick & Jackson, 1971), p. 169.
5. *Hansard*, vol. 670, col. 962 (30 January 1963).
6. *Statement on the Defence Estimates: 1965*, Cmnd 2592, p. 7.

NOTES TO CHAPTER 4

1. Harold Wilson, op. cit., p. 40; Reed and Williams, op. cit., pp. 168–70.
2. Harold Macmillan, *At the End of the Day* (London: Macmillan, 1973), p. 363.
3. *Twelfth Report from the Expenditure Committee*, Session 1972–3, para. 2.
4. 'Polaris Afternoon', *The Economist*, 28 October 1967.
5. *Polaris Sales Agreement*, Cmnd 2108, August 1963.
6. *Hansard*, vol. 748, col. 299 (13 June 1967).
7. Richard Crossman, *The Diaries of a Cabinet Minister*, vol. 3 (London: Hamish Hamilton and Jonathan Cape, 1977) pp. 200, 325.
8. Wilson, op. cit., p. 408.

NOTES TO CHAPTER 5

1. Edward Heath, *Old World, New Horizon: Britain, the Common Market and the Atlantic Alliance* (London: Oxford University Press, 1970) p. 73.
2. The most detailed discussion of this issue is Ian Smart, *Future Conditional: The Prospect for Anglo-French Nuclear Cooperation*, Adelphi Paper No. 78 (London: IISS, 1971).
3. Memorandum from MOD (SCOE 37/1), *Twelfth Report from the Expenditure Committee*, 1972–3.
4. Article IX stated: 'To assure the viability and effectiveness of this Treaty, each party undertakes not to transfer to other states, and not to deploy outside its national territory, ABM systems or their components limited by this treaty.' Both parties agreed that this covered 'technical descriptions and blue-prints'.
5. With Michael Charlton on BBC Radio 4, 16 November 1979.
6. Evidence to the *Twelfth Report from the Expenditure Committee*. For more calculations see Geoffrey Kemp, *Nuclear Forces for Medium Powers*, Part I, *Targets and Weapons Systems*, Parts II and III, *Strategic Requirements and Options*, Adelphi Papers 106 and 107 (London: IISS, 1974).
7. *Hansard*, vol. 977, col. 681 (24 January 1980).
8. *Twelfth Report from the Expenditure Committee*, Session 1972–3, para. 21.

NOTES TO CHAPTER 6

1. See stories by Richard Norton-Taylor in *The Guardian* (11 February and 17 May 1977).

2. *Hansard*, vol. 977, col. 682 (24 January 1980).
3. *Statement on the Defence Estimates: 1975*, Cmnd 5976, para I, 25d.
4. David Fishlock, 'Tritium's place in Britain's nuclear arsenal', *Financial Times*, 15 January 1980.
5. *Twelfth Report from the Expenditure Committee*, Session 1978–9, Evidence, pp. 9, 1. The figures on orders of *Polaris* missiles from the United States come from Department of Defense Security Assistance Agency, *Foreign Military Sales and Military Assistance Facts* (Washington DC: December 1978).
6. Ian Smart, 'Beyond Polaris', *International Affairs* (October 1977), p. 71. His full report was published as *The Future of the British Nuclear Deterrent: Technical, Economic and Strategic Issues* (London: RIIA, 1977).
7. *Hansard*, vol. 946, col. 1315 (21 March 1978).
8. *Hansard* (Lords), vol. 392, col. 601 (18 May 1978).
9. *Sixth Report from the Expenditure Committee*, Session 1978–9, Minutes of Evidence, pp. 1, 7–8, 13. The Prime Minister's views appear in *Hansard*, vol. 960, col. 1500 (16 January 1979).
10. *The Labour Party Manifesto 1979*, pp. 37–8.
11. The existence of these groups and a Cabinet subcommittee was first revealed in Peter Hennessy, 'Planning for a future nuclear deterrent', *The Times* (4 December 1979).
12. *Sixth Report from the Expenditure Committee*, Session 1978–9.
13. *Hansard*, vol. 965, col. 45 (26 March 1979). For an elaboration of Mr Mulley's views once out of office see *Hansard*, vol. 977, cols. 698–700 (24 January 1980).
14. Francis Pym, Speech to Conservative University Students, Nottingham, 26 October 1979.
15. The essence of this movement was reported by David Fairhall, 'UK ready to buy Trident Missiles', *The Guardian*, 1 November 1979.
16. Harold Brown, *Department of Defense Annual Report Fiscal Year 1981* (Washington DC: 29 January 1980), p. 84.
17. Joint Statement issued by President Carter and Prime Minister Margaret Thatcher on 18 December 1979.
18. *Hansard*, vol. 977, col. 774 (24 January 1980).

NOTES TO CHAPTER 7

1. James Bellini and Geoffrey Pattie, *A New World Role for the Medium Power* (London: Royal United Services Institute, 1977).
2. *Hansard*, vol. 936, col. 396 (28 July 1977); vol. 946, cols. 1313–14 (21 March 1978); *Sunday Times*, 18 September 1977.
3. Desmond Ball, 'The Costs of Cruise Missiles', *Survival*, vol. XX, no. 6 (November/December 1978), p. 245.
4. Smart, op. cit., pp. 51–3.
5. *Sixth Report from the Expenditure Committee 1978–79*, Appendix 8, p. 2.
6. David Owen, *The Politics of Defence* (London: Jonathan Cape, 1972) p. 186.

NOTES TO CHAPTER 8

1. *Hansard*, vol. 977, cols. 682–3 (24 January 1980).
2. *Proposed Reduction of United Kingdom Defence Expenditure for 1978/79* (Brussels: NATO 16 September 1977).
3. *Ministerial Guidance 1977*, Annex to the Final Communiqué of the NATO Defence Planning Committee (Brussels: NATO, May 1977).
4. Julian Critchley MP, 'Can Mr Pym defend us any better than Mr Mulley?', *Daily Telegraph*, 24 August 1979.

NOTES TO CHAPTER 9

1. *Hansard*, vol. 884, col. 181 (14 January 1975). The reference to these two sets of negotiations was somewhat strange as neither dealt specifically with strategic forces.
2. In Congressional hearings in March 1978 Rear Admiral Thomas Davies, an Assistant Director of the US Arms Control and Disarmament Agency, described the British point of view as being 'essentially identical with that of the United States'. In response to questioning, he noted a 'tactical' difference over how best to make the treaty multilateral and one other, the details of which were removed by the censor. US Congress House of Representatives, Intelligence and Military Application of Nuclear Energy. Subcommittee of the Armed Services Committee, *Current Negotiations on the Comprehensive Test Ban Treaty* (15 March 1978), pp. 3, 10.
3. Hearings before the Panel on the Strategic Arms Limitation Talks and the Comprehensive Test Ban Treaty of the Intelligence and Military Application on Nuclear Energy Subcommittee of the House of Representatives. Committee on Armed Services, *Effects of a Comprehensive Test Ban Treaty on United States National Security Interests* (14–15 August 1978).

NOTES TO CHAPTER 12

1. Memorandum by Ministry of Defence (SC OE/73/1) *Second Report from the Expenditure Committee*, Session 1975–7, para 32.
2. *Sixth Report from the Expenditure Committee*, Session 1978–9, p. 6.
3. *Speech to Conservative Party Conference*, Blackpool, 9 October 1979.
4. *Hansard*, vol. 977, cols. 678–9 (24 January 1980).
5. The description is that of former US Secretary of Defense, James Schlesinger, taken from a document prepared by the Congressional Research Service, for the Subcommittee on International Security and Scientific Affairs of the House Committee on International Relations on *Authority to Order the Use of Nuclear Weapons* (Washington DC, US GPO, 1975). Britain is discussed on pp. 10–14.
6. *Sixth Report from the Expenditure Committee*, Session 1978–9, p. 129.

7. *Hansard* (House of Lords), vol. 403, col. 1628 (18 December 1979).
8. London: Sidgwick & Jackson, 1978.
9. London: Hamlyn, 1978.
10. Declaration of North Atlantic Council, Ottawa, 19 June 1974.
11. *Hansard*, vol. 977, col. 678 (24 January 1980).
12. *Second Report from the Expenditure Committee*, Session 1975–6 (SCOE 73/1).
13. *Sixth Report from the Expenditure Committee*, Session 1978–9, pp. 119, 129.
14. Roger D. Speed, *Strategic Deterrence in the 1980s* (Stanford, Calif.: Hoover Institution Press, 1979), pp. 121–3.
15. *Hansard*, vol. 977, col. 718 (24 January 1980).
16. *Now*, 9 November 1979, pp. 26, 31, 32.

Index

Acheson, Dean, 16
Airbus, 124
Air defence, 8, 36
   and cruise missiles, 72
Aldermaston, nuclear weapons
   research establishment,
   39–40, 45, 48, 49, 51, 53, 94,
   125
Anglo-American collaboration, 1,
   6–9, 13, 41–3, 66–8, 97
   1958 Agreement, 7, 56
   amended (1959), 7
   reviewed, 42
   see also Nassau; Polaris Sales
      Agreement
Anglo-French collaboration, 14, 43,
   64–6
Antelope/Super Antelope, 39–40, 48, 49
   concept, 48
   see also Chevaline
Anti-ballistic missiles
   problem posed for Britain, 46–7,
   US, 37
   USSR (*Galosh*), 37, 40, 43, 45, 46
   see also Ballistic missile defences
Anti-submarine warfare, xii, 36, 43,
   50–1, 57, 74
   US and USSR compared, 106
Arms control, xv, 61, 86–100, 126, 140
   see also Comprehensive Test Ban;
      Nuclear Non-Proliferation
      Treaty; Partial Test Ban;
      Strategic Arms Limitation
      Talks
Army, British, 33, 80

Athens guidelines, 23, 130
Atlantic Nuclear Force, 23, 25, 29
   see also Multilateral force
Atlas, 8
Atomic Energy Act (US)
   (1946), 6
   (1954), 7
Attlee, Clement, 2

B-1, 70, 107
B-52, 70, 107, 124
Backfire, 107, 110, 113
Ball, Desmond, 151
Ballistic missiles
   compared with bombers, 15
   compared with cruise missiles, 62,
   68, 69–76, 119
   see also ICBMs; SLBMs; *Atlas*; *Blue
      Steel*; *Blue Streak*; *Hound Dog*;
      Jupiter; M-24; *Minuteman*; M-
      X; *Pershing*; *Polaris*; *Poseidon*;
      Skybolt; SS-4; SS-5; SS-16; SS-
      20; *Thor*; *Trident I*; *Trident II*
Ballistic missile defences, 36–7
   see also Anti-ballistic missiles
Barrow, 51, 82
Belgium, 120, 122, 125–6
Bellini, James, 151
   on cruise missiles, 70
Berlin crisis
   (1948), 9
   (1961), 20
Bidwell, Brigadier Shelford, 133
Birkenhead, 51, 82
Blue Steel, 8, 81

Bombers, 70, 107
  see also B-1; B-52; *Buccaneer*;
      Canberra; F-2111; *Harrier*;
      Jaguar, *Mirage IV*; *Tornado*;
      TSR-2; V-bombers
Bourges, Yvon, 65
Brezhnev, President Leonid, 121, 122
British Aerospace Dynamics, 71
  on replacement, 75
British Army of the Rhine, 20, 80
Brown, Harold, 67, 151
Buccaneer, 20
Buis, George, 65

Cabinet Assessment Staff, 60
Callaghan, James, 52, 60, 61, 83, 96
  and Comprehensive Test Ban, 92,
    95
Cameron, Air Marshall Sir Neil, 60,
    124
Campaign for Nuclear Disarmament,
    xiv
Canberra, 20
Cape Canaveral, 54, 147
Carrington, Lord, 44, 62
Carter, President Jimmy, 61, 70, 111,
    151
  and Comprehensive Test Ban, 93,
    95
  and cooperation with Britain, 67, 68
  and neutron bomb, 115, 117
  and SALT, 98, 99, 100
Carver, Lord, on strategic rationales,
    132
Chalfont, Lord, 32
Charlton, Michael, 150
Chevaline, 60, 63, 77, 96
  background, 48
  chosen, 50-1
  cost, 53-4, 55
  and Comprehensive Test Ban, 95
  described, 49
  survives, 53-5
  see also Antelope/Super-Antelope;
    Moscow Criterion; *Polaris*
    SLBM
Chiefs of Staff (Britain), xii, 63, 124
  and Comprehensive Test Ban, 95
  Global Strategy Paper (1952), 3

China, People's Republic of, 37, 88,
    90, 93, 109, 110
Churchill, Sir Winston, 3
Civil Defence, i–ii
Comprehensive Test Ban, 88, 89,
    91-6
Conference on Security and
    Cooperation in Europe
    (CSCE), 87
Conservative Governments
  (1951-64), 3
    and multilateral force, 22-3,
      25, 31
  (1970-4), 42-3, 55
    and future of nuclear force, 43-51
  (1979-),
    and Comprehensive Test Ban,
      95-6
    defence spending, 84-5
    and *Polaris* replacement, 62-3
    SALT, 100
Conservative Party, 26, 66
Conventional forces
  British, 20
  role in deterrence, 12-13, 20, 25,
    102, 105
  see also Flexible response
Cook, Robin, on rationales, 140
Cooper, Sir Frank, 60
Corporal, 20
Critchley, Julian, 152
Crossman, Richard, 39, 150
Cruise missiles, 61, 65, 69-76
  air-launched, 70, 107
  and air defence, 72
  American, 69, 73, 76
  British, 70-1, 73, 75, 79, 123-5
  compared with ballistic missiles, 62,
    68, 69-76, 119
  costs, 71-2
  German (V-1), 69
  ground-launched, xv, 73, 119, 121,
    122, 124, 126
  and NATO's theatre nuclear forces,
    119-26
  and SALT, 97-9
  sea-launched, 74, 75
  see also Mace-B; SS-N-3
Cuban Missile Crisis, 16, 31, 101

Davies, Rear Admiral Thomas, 152
'De-coupling', 103–5, 118, 124
Defence budget (British), 82–5
   and nuclear force, 32, 53, 57, 79–82,
      85, 134–5, 139, 144, 145
Defence Review (1975), 53, 54, 83
De Gaulle, President Charles, 16, 24,
   39
Denmark, 122
Deterrence, theory of, xii, 27–8,
      102–5, 127–35
   in 1950s, 3–4
   and British Nuclear Force, 19
   European views on, 12, 104–5
   and Kennedy Administration,
      11–12, 19–20
   and neutron bomb, 115
   and theatre nuclear forces, 118
   see also De-coupling; Escalation;
         Flexible response; Limited
         nuclear war; Moscow
         Criterion; Proportionality;
         Rationales; Sanctuary
         strategy; Second-decision
         centre; Trigger theory; US
         Nuclear Guarantee
Double-key system, 114, 119–20
Douglas-Home, Sir Alec, 88
Duff, Sir Anthony, 60, 63
Dulles, John Foster, 4

The Economist, on *Polaris* force, 37–8
Eisenhower, President Dwight D., 7,
   21
'Escalation', 21, 27, 29, 104–5, 124,
   131
   escalation dominance, 112
   see also Limited nuclear war
European Communities, i, 38
   British attempts at entry, 1, 14, 16,
      39, 40, 42, 139
   British entry, 41, 66, 101
European nuclear force, 14, 42, 138–9
Expenditure Committee, House of
      Commons, 49, 59, 75, 136
   on nuclear policy, 50, 61

F-111, 111, 123, 125
Fairhall, David, 151

Faslane, 35, 77
Fishlock, David, 151
Flexible response, 20, 29, 104
Ford, President Gerald, 98
Foreign and Commonwealth Office,
      60, 75, 76
   and Comprehensive Test Ban, 95
France, 22, 25, 29, 72, 88, 93, 97, 101,
      111, 127, 133, 140
   and Germany, 65
   nuclear forces, 14, 64
   theory of deterrence, 23–4
   and US, 13–14, 67

Gaitskell, Hugh, 31
Genscher, Hans-Dietrich, 115
Germany
   East, 121
   Nazi, 1
   West, 42, 101, 115, 116, 134, 138
   and multilateral force, 22
   and cruise missiles, 99
   and neutron bomb, 116–17
   and theatre nuclear forces, 10,
      118–21, 123, 125, 126
Giscard d'Estaing, President Valery,
   65
Gordon Walker, Patrick, 31
Goronway-Roberts, Lord, on
      Comprehensive Test Ban, 92
Gowing, Margaret, 149
Gray, Colin, 143
Greece, 120
Groom, John, 149
Guadeloupe Summit, 61

Hackett, Sir John, 132
Harrier, 84
Hayhoe, Barney, 68
Healey, Denis, 31–2, 34, 52, 60
   on strategic rationale, 26, 127
Heath, Edward, 45, 150
   on European nuclear force, 42
Hennessy, Peter, 151
Holland, 42
   and neutron bomb, 116
   and theatre nuclear forces, 120–1,
      122, 125–6

Holy Loch, 9, 67
Honest John, 20
'Hot line', 31
Hound Dog, 17
Howe, Sir Geoffrey, 62
Hunt, Sir John, 60

Iceland, 121
'Independence' of British nuclear
        force, 5–6, 16, 17–18, 25,
        137–8
India
    and British nuclear guarantee of,
        28–9
    own nuclear device, 89
Intercontinental ballistic missiles
        (ICBM's)
    American, 15, 26, 72
    American and Soviet compared,
        106–7
    ICBM vulnerability, 107–8, 112
    in SALT, 97
    Soviet, 10–11
    see also Atlas; *Minuteman*; M-X;
        SS-16
International Atomic Energy
        Authority, 89
International Institute for Strategic
        Studies, 49
Israel, 89
Italy, and Theatre Nuclear Forces,
        120–1, 126

Jaguar, 84
Jenkins, Roy, 52
Johnson, President Lyndon, 38
Jupiter, 118

Kemp, Geoffrey, 150
Kennedy, President John, 11, 12, 20,
        21, 23, 66, 149
    at Nassau, 16
Kennedy, Senator Edward, 68
Kerr, Dr Donald, on Britain and Test
        Ban, 94
Khruschev, Nikita, 11
Kissinger, Dr Henry, 43, 51, 70
    on British rejection of *Poseidon*, 46

Labour Governments,
    (1945–51), 2–3
    (1964–70), 23, 28–9, 31–40, 42
        and India, 26
        and MIRVs, 51
        and Multilateral Force, 20
    (1974–9), 51
        and *Chevaline*, 52–5
        and Comprehensive Test Ban,
            93–4
        and defence budget, 83
        and *Polaris* replacement, 55,
            58–62
Labour Party, xiv
    1964 Manifesto, 24–5
    1975 Manifestos, 59, 87
Lance, 114
Latin America nuclear-free zone, 87,
        89
Lewin, Admiral Sir Terence, 63
'Limited nuclear war', 21, 105, 110,
        112, 135
    see also Escalation
Lockheed, 55, 56
Luns, Dr Joseph, on British defence
        budget, 83–4
Luxembourg, 120

M-4, 64
Mace-B, 119
McGovern, Senator George, 44
Macmillan, Harold, 150
    on cost of *Polaris*, 33
    at Nassau, 16–18, 25
    on rationale, 5, 28
McNamara, Robert, 12, 15, 33
    on independent nuclear deterrents,
        13, 19
Manhattan Project, 1
Mason, Ronald, 60, 63, 71
Mason, Roy, 52, 54
    on arms control, 87
Ministry of Defence,
    attitude to multilateral force, 22, 38
    and Comprehensive Test Ban, 92,
        94
    and cruise missiles, 71, 75, 76,
        123–5

Ministry of Defence (*cont.*)
  on costs of *Polaris*, 57
  and rationales, 127, 136
  on replacements, 59, 60, 61–2, 63,
    77
Minuteman, 15
Mirage IV, 14, 64
Monte Bello, 1
'Moscow Criterion', 47, 54, 60
  see also Chevaline
Mountbatten, Lord Louis, 17
Mulley, Fred, 54, 60, 61, 65, 151
  on cruise missile studies, 71,
  on *Polaris*, 57
  on rationales, 128
  on replacement, 58–9, 59, 62
Multilateral force, 21–3, 25, 29, 115,
    116
Multiple independently targeted re-
    entry vehicles (MIRVs), 36,
    37, 65, 97
  and Britain, 39, 51
Mutual and Balanced Force
    Reductions Talks, 87, 109
M-X, 106, 108

Nassau, Summit, 15–18, 28, 32, 38,
    41, 79
  agreement, 17–18, 22, 24, 25, 33,
    98, 101
  see also Anglo-American
    collaboration
Neustadt, Professor Richard, 149
Neutron bomb, 65, 98, 114–17, 118,
    122
Nevada test site, 91, 96
Nixon, President Richard, 43, 44, 70
Non-Proliferation Act (US), 90
North Atlantic Treaty Organisation
    (NATO), xiv, 1
  and British defence effort, 82–4,
    134–5
  and British nuclear force, 25, 26
  and cruise missiles, 98
  long-term defence programme, 84,
    111
  and nuclear weapons, 102–5
  see also Nuclear Planning Group;
    Deterrence theory

Norton-Taylor, Richard, 150
Norway, 120
Nuclear Non-Proliferation Treaty, 23,
    88, 89–91, 93
  Article VI, 90
Nuclear Planning Group, 23, 98, 111,
    121, 140
  High Level Group of, 111, 118, 121
Nuclear tests, 91
  by Britain, 52, 55–6, 91, 148
  see also Proof tests; Nevada test site

Owen, Dr David, 54, 60, 61, 75, 151
  on independent deterrent, 75

Pakistan, 89
Palliser, Sir Michael, 60
Partial Test Ban Treaty, 31, 88, 91
Pattie, Geoffrey, 151
  on cruise missiles, 70
  on rationale, 132, 137
Pershing, 119, 121, 124, 126
Pierre, Andrew, 149, 150
Polaris sales agreement, 38, 99
Polaris submarines
  American, 9, 22, 26, 35, 42, 56, 80
  British, xii, 32, 43, 80
  characteristics, 142
  cost, 33, 144, 145
  fifth boat, 26, 31, 33–7, 44, 75
  launch procedures, xiii–xiv, 35
  long re-fits, 34–5, 43, 57, 80
  obsolescence, 57–8
  operating pattern, xii–xiv, 34–5, 44
  Repulse, 34, 142, 147
  Resolution, 34, 35, 43, 64, 65, 142, 147
  Revenge, 34, 142, 147
Polaris SLBM
  American, 15, 42
    characteristics, 143
    A-1, 38, 48
    A-32, 35, 38, 48
    A-3, 36, 38, 48
  British, xii, 26, 37, 39, 46, 74, 75, 77,
    79, 85, 95, 110, 123, 133
    and arms control, 87–8, 91
    capabilities, 32, 36, 55
    characteristics, 143

chosen in 1962, 17–18
cost, 82, 144, 145
not chosen in 1960, 16–17
obsolescence, 56–7
purchases from US, 32–3, 57
replacement, 54, 56–68, 81, 86
tests, 146
'upgraded *Polaris*', 63, 76
see also Chevaline
Poniatowski, Michel, 65
Poseidon SLBM
American, 37, 38, 111
capabilities, 37, 48, 143
British
discussed in 1967, 38–40
discussed in 1972–3, 45–51, 53, 54
Proof tests, 94, 95
Proportionality, 24, 132
Pym, Francis, 125, 133, 151
on *Chevaline*, 49, 62, 67, 79
on rationales, 128–9, 136
on replacement, 63, 64, 81

Rationales
as contribution to NATO, 25, 26, 127, 134–5
as insurance policy, 135–9
outside of NATO, 28–30
political, 139–40
strategic, 5, 13–14, 24, 28–30, 55, 127–39
see also Independence; Moscow Criterion; Proportionality; Sanctuary strategy; Second-decision centre; Trigger theory
Reed, Bruce, 150
Rickover, Admiral Hyman, 42
Rodgers, William, on replacement issue, 68
Rose, Sir Clive, 60
Rosyth, 34
Royal Air Force, 4, 17, 33, 80
and cruise missiles, 71
Royal Navy, 80
and fifth boat, 34
and multilateral force, 22
and nuclear force, 17
and *Poseidon*, 38, 45, 49

'Sanctuary' strategy, 27, 135
Sandys, Duncan, 20
on deterrence, 4
Sanguinetti, Alexandre, 65
Satellites, 65, 72
Schlesinger, James, 152
'Second-decision centre', 26–7, 30, 127–34
Seismic detectors, 93
and Britain, 96
Simpson, Dr John, 149
Singapore, 29
Single Integrated Operation Plan, 26
Skybolt, 81
British decision to buy, 8–9
US rejects, 15–16
Smart, Ian, 142, 150, 151
on cruise missiles, 74–5
on replacement issue, 58
South Africa, 89
South Korea, 2, 89
Soviet Union
on British and French forces, 97, 133
build-up of forces, 105–6
and Comprehensive Test Bans, 92, 93, 96
and limited nuclear war, 105, 110
on NATO nuclear forces, 116, 121–2
on nuclear Germany, 99
vulnerability to British forces, 32, 36
Speed, Dr Roger, 152
Sputnik, 10
SS-4, 109
SS-5, 109
SS-16, 110
SS-20, 64, 110, 112–13, 115, 122
SS-N-3, 67, 70
Strategic Air Command, 25, 26
Strategic Arms Limitation Talks (SALT), 44, 59, 88, 91, 96, 96–100, 106, 109, 116, 117
ABM Treaty, 44–5, 47, 72–3, 96
and cruise missiles, 70, 97–8, 119
non-transfer clauses, 44, 98–9, 117, 150
and offensive arms, 44, 50, 96–7
SALT II, 86, 97–100

Strategic Arms Talks (*cont.*)
  and theatre nuclear forces, 113, 116,
    121, 126
Submarines, 74
  and cruise missiles, 74–5
  diesel versus nuclear power, 77–8
  dual-capable, 75–6
Submarine-launched ballistic missiles
    (SLBMs),
  in SALT, 97
  as theatre nuclear forces, 111, 118
  US and Soviet compared, 106–7
  see also M-4; *Polaris*; *Poseidon*; *Trident
    I*; *Trident II*
Suez, 5, 24
  'nuclear Suez', 25

Tactical nuclear weapons, and NATO
    strategy, 10, 20, 21, 130–1
  see also Theatre nuclear forces
Taiwan, 89
Tercom, 70, 71, 71–2
Thatcher, Margaret, xiii, 62, 67, 151
  and SALT, 100
Theatre nuclear forces, long-range
  British, 110–11, 120, 123–5, 126
  NATO, xiv, 61, 62, 105, 108,
    110–11, 113, 117–26
  and arms control, 121–2
  and flexible response, 20, 118
  Soviet, 22, 105, 108, 109–10
  see also F-111; *Jupiter*; *Pershing*; SS-4;
    SS- ; SS-20; *Thor*; Cruise
    missiles
Thor, 110
Thorneycroft, Lord, 33
Tinajero, A.A., 143
Tornado, 49, 81, 99, 123, 124, 125
Treasury, 32, 34, 54, 60, 63, 78
Trident I SLBM, 50, 63, 67, 68, 76–7,
    81, 85, 86, 107, 125
  British purchase of, 67–8, 100
  capabilities, 77, 143
Trident II SLBM, 107
'Trigger' theory, 25, 131, 132
Tritium, 56
Trotter, Neville, on US nuclear
    guarantee, 136

Truman, President Harry S., 2
TSR-2, 81, 123
Turkey, 110, 120

United Nations, special session on
    disarmament, 92
United States
  bases in Britain, 87, 125, 135
  and British nuclear forces, 43, 66–7
  and Comprehensive Test Ban, 92,
    93–6
  Congress, 6, 46, 67
  Defence Department, 67
  and multilateral force, 21–3
  and neutron bomb, 115
  US Navy, 38, 45
  and SALT, 96–100
US nuclear guarantee, 10
  and Britain, 13, 21, 27, 29, 129,
    136–7
  and France, 23–4, 27, 103
  and ICBM vulnerability, 107–8
  and NATO, 101, 102–3
  see also Deterrence theory; North
    Atlantic Treaty Organisation

V-Bombers, 8, 14, 23, 25, 29, 43, 99,
    144
  Valiants, 26, 123
  Victors, 26, 123
  Vulcans, 26, 111, 123–4

Warsaw Pact, 26, 102
  and tactical nuclear weapons, 10
Wass, Sir Douglas, 60
Whitelaw, William, 62
Wigg, George, 32
Williams, Geoffrey, 150
Wilson, Sir Harold, 31, 40, 52, 149,
    150
  guarantee to India, 28–9
  on independent deterrent, 25
  on *Poseidon*, 38–9
  on 1964 decision-making, 32
Windscale, 90
Winterbottom, Lord, on *Polaris*
    replacement, 59